UNFORGETTABLE
Life's Journey

UNFORGETTABLE
Life's Journey
The True Memoir of an African Child

Prince A. Cummings

iUniverse®

UNFORGETTABLE LIFE'S JOURNEY
THE TRUE MEMOIR OF AN AFRICAN CHILD

iUniverse books may be ordered through booksellers or by contacting:

iUniverse
1663 Liberty Drive
Bloomington, IN 47403
www.iuniverse.com
1-800-Authors (1-800-288-4677)

Because of the dynamic nature of the Internet, any web addresses or links contained in this book may have changed since publication and may no longer be valid. The views expressed in this work are solely those of the author and do not necessarily reflect the views of the publisher, and the publisher hereby disclaims any responsibility for them.

Any people depicted in stock imagery provided by Getty Images are models, and such images are being used for illustrative purposes only. Certain stock imagery © Getty Images.

ISBN: 978-1-5320-6114-1 (sc)
ISBN: 978-1-5320-6113-4 (e)

Library of Congress Control Number: 2018913600

Print information available on the last page.

iUniverse rev. date: 11/21/2018

Contents

I personally dedicate this book to my late mother, Josephine Abie Shodeke, and my late mother-in-law, Mabinty Kargbo. To our lovely granddaughter Kaira Mary Abioseh Princess Cummings. In addition, to all our youths in Sierra Leone who are determined to succeed in life so that they too can contribute to national development.

Acknowledgements

Firstly, let me thank God, my Maker, for giving me good health and continued strength to enable me to write this book. I am blessed that this book has finally become a reality. This is a wonderful opportunity for me to be able to share my story with others. I believe that my story will influence others, especially youths, in a positive way.

I would like to take this special opportunity to thank my immediate family members: my wife, Florella, and my children, Sylvanus, Marcus, Sia, and Jessica. They have all played their roles in ensuring that this book was completed. I thank my aunty Rosa and other family members and friends for their support as I sailed through.

I also want to thank my publishing team at iUniverse for their tremendous support in taking me through all the steps and ensuring that the final product was perfect. Special thanks to Mitchel and Jill for their personal contact and support throughout the entire process.

Finally, thanks to my house support staff, Sorie and Hawa, for creating an enabling environment for me to sit and write this book.

Chapter 1

Childhood and Growing Up

Growing up was an interesting part of my life. Many things happen while one is growing up and experiencing childhood. My childhood was full of challenges but at the same time a lot of excitement.

I grew up with my maternal grandparents, the late Joseph Johnson and Modu Johnson of 16 Fleck Street, Waterloo. My grandfather was the head of the Waterloo Post Service Company, as it was known at the time. I grew up with my younger brother Davidson, now deceased, and two of my cousins, Adolphus and Tobias, all of us living together in the same house under the supervision of our grandparents. Also two of my younger uncles stayed with us in that house: Uncle Prince, now deceased, and Uncle Johnathan. The house was a traditional residence made with mud bricks and timber windows. It had four bedrooms. I and two of my cousins occupied one room. We had a small back yard with various plantations, including coconut, banana, and mango trees, to name a few. Located at the back of the house was the toilet. The house was in the middle of the property and shared boundaries with two other houses, one on each side—our neighbours. We had various house rules that everyone had to follow and obey if they truly wanted to be part of the family. It was compulsory to obey the rules; otherwise, there was a series of punishments prescribed by our grandparents. Every child knows what he or she needs to do on a daily basis to avoid being seriously punished by those in authority.

We were four in number, all grandchildren. Our grandmother was pleased to have us in the house, but she was also determined that each one of us should attend school and get the best education possible. She had been educated to the high school level but was clever and highly intelligent. She was always there to sacrifice her time and put forth her effort to ensure our schoolwork was done.

I recall one particular day, one of the usual public holidays when we were allowed to go out and interact with other children in the neighbourhood. Before leaving the house, we got a strict warning from our grandfather reminding us that we needed to be home before 6 p.m. He specifically told us that when we saw the hair on our hands laying down, it was a sign that it was getting late and we needed to return home. We left home that afternoon to watch a cultural performance involving masks that was taking place about two miles away from our house. I and my cousins arrived at the scene of the show, and everyone got excited. The show was well attended, and the place was crowded.

My cousins and I were so focused on the show that we completely forgot about the instructions given to us by our grandpa to return before 6 p.m. We even failed to observe the signs, neglecting to look at the hair on our hands laying down, an indicator that night was coming. We'd met some of our school friends and were overcome by the dancing and other amusements. When I finally came to the realization that it was getting dark and we needed to return home, I couldn't find my cousins. I spent some time looking for them and eventually found them. We left for the house. It was already dark. We knew in our minds that we had violated the rules, and for sure we were going to be punished. So we braced ourselves for the worst. Eventually we arrived home well past 6 p.m. We met our grandpa outside on the veranda, where he was waiting for us.

We greeted him, and he answered slowly and asked us to stand and wait. We already knew what was going to be the consequence, and we were ready for it. Then the moment came. He stood up from his seated position and asked, "What did I say to you all when you were leaving this house?" My younger brother Davidson was always the bravest to act and speak on our behalf. He started explaining and trying to make up some stories. My grandpa was furious and disturbed. He raised his voice, saying, "So you all decided to disobey my instructions and did what you wanted to do?" He already had the flogging stick beside his chair; it was meant to be used to punish all three of us. He finally asked each of us to kneel down. Once we did, he administered a dozen strokes to each one of us and then asked us to take a cold bath before entering the house. That is a moment I will never forget. It exemplifies the type of discipline our grandparents gave us when it came to setting a good example. After that event, none of us ever attempted to repeat that same mistake.

As a young boy growing up, I, along with my cousins at home, had a series of responsibilities that strictly needed to be carried out as dictated by our grandmother. For example, every individual was assigned a particular day when it was his or her turn to grind dry pepper, onion, and Benin seed, usually called Ogiri in our Creole language. In the event that it was your day to do the task and it was not done, you would be punished severely. One of the punishments was that you were provided with half a meal that day. In addition, depending on our grandfather's mood, you could be flogged. In essence, everyone made sure they took their responsibilities seriously when it came to house chores and duties.

Failing to do any of those chores was a punishable act. So everyone made sure they took their housework seriously. And we took no chances, because the consequences were great. The same went for schoolwork and homework. Each of us children ensured that we woke up early in the morning, did our household work, and got ready for school. After school, we ensured we arrived home on time. Failure to arrive on time without any valid excuse would result in punishment. Everyone knew what the consequences were for breaking household rules and for being defiant.

Our grandparents knew exactly what was right and wrong for our upbringing, and they spent many hours with us explaining how young boys like us growing up should behave both at home and outside the home. It was mandatory that all of us follow their instructions to the letter. There was no room for disobedience or disrespect, not even among us as peers. Our elders needed to be respected, and in turn younger ones needed to be protected. It was forbidden in those days for young a person to disrespect an elder at home or outside the home.

If a young child was accused of disrespecting an elderly person, such young person would be severely dealt with. In most cases, he or she would be punished by other older people in the community, even before the child got home.

In fact, back then it was the young person's responsibility to report himself to his parents or guardians when he arrived home. In most cases young people like me in those days would even refuse to complain once we got home, the reason being that ten chances to one, we would be liable to be punished again by our parents or guardian. The role of elders in our communities was one deserving of the utmost respect. It was they who set forth the principles for a peaceful and accommodating society for everyone. All had responsibility for ensuring a child in the community would grow up with dignity and respect. It was a communal responsibility and not just the responsibility of biological relatives.

There was a sense of belonging from all and for each other in the community. Everyone was known to the others in the communities in which we lived. It was easy to identify strangers who came to visit our communities in those days. It was also easy to know when something happened, be it good or bad. In either event, everyone would support each other and stay together. Everyone was focused on caring for one another, especially children growing up in the community. A child when seen doing anything within the community that was not right would be corrected immediately by another person in the community, either by chastising the child or giving her some punishment that would make sure she would never repeat such an act. There was a sense of obligation to each other regardless of where you came from, your political leaning, or the position you held in society. Everyone came together to make sure things worked. Because of this, young people like us were very serious about our studies and with our books. We knew what everyone wanted when we attended school, and we knew what sort of accomplishments everyone was aiming at.

In my view, and looking back now from this vantage point, I can say that a child was well cared for and monitored in the community and at school. Each child was taught to emulate the fine principles of discipline, to respect everyone, and to become a good citizen in his community. In fact, it was very rare to see a young person misbehave in public. Children were aware of the consequences they would face both at the community level and at home. All family members wanted to protect the good name of their families, so they worked hard to ensure that their children were well brought up and had respect for all.

Apart from all the challenges that life itself brings when one is growing up, there were other interesting aspects that I will share. One of these interesting aspects was living in the same house with my cousins. Not only that, but also having other children in the neighbourhood with whom we all grew up. We played, shared food, and sometimes even studied together outside. For our studies, especially late in the evenings, many of us would converge under the street lights to read under the guidance of an elder or a teacher within the community. It was interesting to see how we all interacted with each other and provided support for one another in the community setting. As children, we shared responsibilities and helped one another to become good boys and girls in the community. We had the same type of support from young people who were older than we.

It was a system of belonging, and there was no segregation between Muslims and Christians. We held things in common regardless of tribe, status, or religious background. We were all together. During Christmastime, my family home was a dedicated Seventh-Day Adventist home, but we did observe the Christmas celebration and ensured we sent out food to all our neighbours as a sign of gratitude, appreciation, and above all, love and caring. It was the same for our Muslim neighbours. They would send us food during the Ramadan celebration. The concerns for one another went beyond neighbourliness.

They went much farther than that. When there were difficult times within the neighbourhood, for example the death of a family member, there was always the support of the neighbours and the rest of the community. There was a sense of togetherness and a oneness. When there were celebrations like weddings, the entire community would join hands to support the newlyweds. Nothing was done without the consent of the other neighbours.

As a child growing up, I had this attitude of love and caring drilled into me. All of us children shared the same love and concern for our peers in the neighbourhood. We fetched water together from streams and street pipes. We went out in the forest together to fetch firewood. It was like a habit that just developed in us. Every child within the communities cherished those moments when we carried out household chores for our various parents.

I remember a particular event. In the morning we had groups who would wake up as early as five o'clock and go round the community at various points to search for mangoes. Mango trees were plentiful in various open plots that were left unattended. There were also mango trees located within our neighbours' yards. Waking up early in the morning was a disadvantage for the group who made it to any mango grove first. Once there, they were sure to collect many mangoes from the ground. In most cases these mangoes were taken to school to be sold to schoolmates or teachers. This was how many of us got our lunch money and earned some pocket money.

One particular time when I and my cousins were going to go out to search for mangoes, we awoke very early. If I'm not mistaken, it was 4 a.m. We approached one of the mango trees only to see a shadow in white sitting beneath it. We believed this was a ghost. Ghosts are dead people who come out of their graves at night-time. No sooner had we seen the white object than we were all convinced it was a ghost waiting for us. We dropped our bowls and fled the area. While we were running, the object was following us. That was one day in my life when I ran as if my entire being was going to come out of me. After we had gone quite a distance, the object stopped at some point and started laughing and pointing in our direction. It was afterwards that we realized it was one of our friends from one of the other groups who'd decided to pretend to be a ghost just to scare us and collect our mangoes. There were several more events like this that I enjoyed growing up.

I was a very quiet child, and my cousins usually would take advantage of that and bully me. Most of the bullying was specifically geared towards getting me to give them my share of the food at home. They understood I was quiet and that I rarely complained, so they took advantage of that situation. Inasmuch as I was quiet, I also made sure that people wouldn't take advantage of me all the time. I was concerned about other young boys my age also taking advantage of me. But I stood firm for what I knew was right and would always fight back in instances when I knew that my peers wanted to take advantage of me.

I always longed for Fridays to come. I had been taught by my grandparents to respect the Sabbath Day as it is the day our good Lord has created for us to rest. It is a day to be observed according to Exodus 20:8 in the Bible: "Remember the Sabbath day and keep it holy." The Sabbath actually starts on Friday evening at sunset. This was when I, my cousins, and the entire household would make sure that we made all our preparations. Some of the things we did to prepare for the Sabbath on Friday included cooking food, ironing our church clothes, cleaning our shoes, sweeping, and ensuring the compound and surroundings were clean.

All of that was done on Friday in preparation for the next day, the Sabbath, when we attended church and worshipped our God. My cousins and I were always excited for Friday and Saturday, the latter being the Sabbath Day. No work was done in the house on Saturday. We spent almost the entire day in church attending service and then going to a programme for young people like us. A lot was being taught in our children's classes. I had lots of friends whom I attended school with. The Sabbath was a day for us to dress well and attend church and other meetings. We had missionaries who loved children, and they taught us a lot from the Bible, especially the love that Jesus demonstrated to us while he was here on earth.

In those classes we were taught to obey our parents and the elderly in our communities and in the church. These are values that as a child were instilled in me. I grew up knowing how to discipline myself. I always got along well with the elders in my community and church. One other interesting point to note is that, as a child, if you were seen outside your home doing something you weren't supposed to be doing, elders in the community would be the first to discipline you before you reached home. If you were not careful, you could rest assured that your parents would add their own part of the punishment if they found out what you'd done from those neighbours or elders.

Chapter 2

My Parents

My parents are both natives of Waterloo Town. Waterloo is a city in the Western Area of Sierra Leone and is the capital of the Western Area Rural District, which is one of the fourteen districts of Sierra Leone. Located about fifteen miles east of Freetown, Waterloo is the second-largest city in the Western Area region of Sierra Leone, after Freetown. The city had a population of 34,079 according to the 2004 census and an estimated population of 40,000 in 2013. Waterloo is part of the Freetown metropolitan area.

Waterloo is a major urban transport hub and lies on the main highway linking Freetown to the country's provinces. Waterloo lies about twenty miles to the east of the Port Loko District in the Northern Province.

Waterloo is one of Sierra Leone's most ethnically diverse cities, as it is home to many of Sierra Leone's ethnic groups, with no single ethnic group forming the majority of the population. The Krio people are the principal inhabitants of Waterloo, and they are politically influential in the city. The Krio language is by far the most widely spoken language in the city.

Although Waterloo is part of the larger Western Area Rural District Council, the city has its own directly elected town council headed by a town head.

My mother, Josephine Abie Shodeke née Johnson (now deceased), was a hard-working and loving mother. She was an educationist and served as a teacher and head teacher for thirty-nine years. She was very strict and always wanted the best for her children. My mother made a tremendous sacrifice in raising me and my brothers and sister amid difficult circumstances. I was the oldest of four siblings, Davidson (deceased), Regina, and Achiebald all being younger than I. My mother was a college student when I was young and had to shuttle between college and home. She did all sorts of odd jobs to ensure she could provide for me and my siblings. Many thanks to her sisters and brothers who also supported us. My uncle Sylvanus, my late aunty Ayo, and my aunty Rosa all played vital roles in supporting her during those trying times. My mother was a fighter and a woman of virtue and high morals. She was a role model for her peers and friends, and they always looked up to her for advice and support. Her determination and admiration are two of the motivating factors that triggered me to write this book.

My mother was a fighter and was always there to teach us children to respect our elders and behave well in our community. She also taught us to be disciplined anywhere we found ourselves. Several times she actually scolded me and my brother for doing things which were totally wrong and unacceptable. She also taught us to be content and humble. We grew up satisfied with what we had. We had very few sets of clothes, and they were all meant for different occasions. We had clothing for church, for outside occasions, and for daily use. It was totally forbidden to mix any pieces of this clothing. We were very satisfied with the few material things we had, and we cherished them. My mother taught me how to make several cookies and cakes to sell during school hours. I took advantage of learning this skill and baked several cookies and cakes, including my favourite, banana bread.

My Father, Ade Cummings, is a fine gentleman who also wanted the best for me and my late brother Davidson Cummings. He is humble and very accommodating. He likes family and always supports us when he can. My father worked in various institutions, including the police force of Sierra Leone, which was his first job ever. After leaving the police force, he worked for the American Embassy as a senior driver and supervisor in charge of all the relief food provided for schools and hospitals supported by the United States Agency for International

Development (USAID). Because of his diligence, hard work, and commitment, he became very popular among his colleagues, to the point where he was nicknamed "Ambassador". Even today many of his friends and colleagues know him by that name. He currently lives at Waterloo and is enjoying what remains of his old age.

I grew up with little knowledge of my father. I was not close to him, and neither was my brother, because we did not live together. My siblings and I only had the opportunity to visit our father once every month at his house at Waterloo. He was a busy and popular man and spent quite a lot of time travelling from one district to another serving the American Embassy in the bid to supply food to primary schools.

Remember that I was the eldest in a family of four. Being the eldest, I grew up with my grandparents, together with my late brother Davidson. Later I had the opportunity to settle down with my mother for a few years when she eventually got married to my stepfather David Shodeke, who is now deceased. My sister Regina and my brother Achie also stayed with our grandparents for some time after I and my cousins left for different locations to attend to our studies. Achie actually spent more time with my maternal grandparents. This was when he started his high school in Waterloo Town.

On my father's side, I have other brothers and sisters. One of them, Princess, is older than I. She also grew up in Waterloo and stayed with my paternal grandparents for many years. She knew more of my relatives from my father's side of the family than I did.

I lived in Waterloo for several years, up to the end of my primary education, staying with my maternal grandparents and, in some instances, with my mother. At the end of my primary education, I did my first year at the Peninsular Secondary School at Waterloo. It had always been my ambition to attend the Methodist Boys High School in Freetown. At the end of my first year, I got a very good result that allowed me to gain entrance to the Methodist Boys High School with the help of my aunt Rosa Johnson. My aunt Rosa was an educationist and was very strict. When I was accepted at the Methodist Boys High

School, I had to relocate to Freetown to stay with my aunt Rosa, who was living at Kissy at that time, close to my school. It was a walking distance of about twenty-five minutes to my school.

It was a pleasant time, having to start a new life and live in the city. My aunty Rosa was a strict disciplinarian, and it took me some time to come to understand her and her behaviour. Sometimes her actions towards me made me see her more as a large problem than a helper. But gradually I came to understand her very well, and we did get along most of the time. I learnt many things from her. Today I am proud of those moments when I felt she was too much of a pest to me. I am now reaping the benefits. This is also a lesson for those who live with distant relatives or guardians and are going through such things. It is important to note that most of what is taught to us is for our own good and will go a long way in the future to help us in our career paths.

Chapter 3

School Days

As the saying goes, school days are the best of times. I would like to confirm this statement by adding that school days not only are the best but also bring moments of peace, joy, friendship, and determination. When I was a student, I realized that life was not just about attending school, making friends, and taking classes. My school days were a time when I needed to make certain decisions for myself that would determine my success or failure in the future. I quickly grasped the concept of having to make certain decisions that would see me through life.

My primary school education was at the Seventh-Day Adventist School, Waterloo Village. I completed my primary education after earning a passing grade on what was called the Selective Entrance Examination, which is completed in class 7. I passed this to gain entrance to Peninsular Secondary School in Waterloo and started with my new form, which was form 1A. At the end of the first year I transferred to the Methodist Boys High School in Kissy Mess, Freetown. It had always been my dream to attend the Methodist Boys High School (MBHS), for several reasons. One of the major reasons was the school band and scout movement that the school held in high esteem.

I finally made it to MBHS and was placed in a class called 2B. When I transferred there, I had to stay and live with my aunt, my mother's younger sister, who was an educationist. She was teaching in a school called Sierra Leone Muslim Congress, which was just few metres away from MBHS, which I was attending. This was interesting because my aunt was very familiar with the MBHS system, so it was difficult for me to play truant.

I started my first day of school with zeal and determination, knowing well that MBHS had high standards and tough competition. This meant I needed to be more serious and pay more attention to my studies and marks. I took second position from form one in my previous school to qualify for entrance into MBHS. I convinced myself that with hard work, I would surely succeed and make it to the next form. My first week was very interesting. It was the week that I got to know most of the school system and the teachers and to meet some new friends and colleagues.

This was also the week when the school carried out what is popularly known as "refresher student initiation" for new students. Some of my friends had mentioned the process and how it was done, but they hadn't mentioned to me how serious it would be or the numerous opportunities for fun it created for the older students. The initiation was to be carried out within the school premises on a Friday. The process was quite interesting and orderly, carried out by senior boys with few teachers involved.

It was during the afternoon, just a little after one o'clock, when everyone was called to assemble in front of the teachers at the principal's office. During this period, all those who were newcomers were directed to remain at the front of the assembly. No one was allowed to move away from a particular demarcated area. The older students surrounded us new students. The entire process took about ten minutes.

There was lot of singing going on. At some point all the newcomers were asked to close their eyes. You were punished if you were caught with your eyes open. At the point when the singing was going on, the school band was playing. And then from out of nowhere, water with mixed with green leaves was poured on every new student. It was very frustrating to endure that, but it gave us new students the opportunity to be called full-fledged members (complete with membership numbers) of MBHS. After going through the process, we were fully recognized as members and students of MBHS.

This process made you proud and led you to believe that you were now part of the great Methodist Boys High School. Before, when you were not initiated, you were called a greener, meaning you were a new student who had not been fully initiated into the school system. After undergoing the initiation process, you got an opportunity the following year to demonstrate your right as an older boy to do the same to other boys just joining the school.

At MBHS, I was one of the proudest among the thousands of high school boys who attended. The school was well established by the Methodist Church and had served the nation in many ways. We heard of many students who had served in several capacities in the country and had contributed a lot towards nation-building.

At the school I was a member of the choir, the scout movement, and the band. I was one of those students who was outstanding and served the school in various capacities. I was well known by almost all of the teachers and of course the principal at the time, Mr Willie O. Pratt, who is now deceased.

Mr Pratt was a mentor to me, and we actually get along well. A father figure to me, he showed me he was a true disciplinarian. He was also the school's deputy bandmaster at the time, and for some reason he was very interested in me. He was the one who actually introduced me to trumpet and eventually took it upon himself to train and teach me and several of my classmates how to play the trumpet. We usually spent one or two hours after school practising and learning how to play several instruments. Most of the time Mr Pratt would be around to give us direction. Mr Pratt knew music and played several other instruments, but his main instruments were cornet and trumpet. I finally completed my training after about four months and was then given the opportunity to start playing with the band. It was an exciting time when I started. I felt so proud that finally I would play the trumpet and join my colleagues to march and play with the great MBHS band. The school band was a symbol of success and service to the school and the nation.

The school band played for various engagements, ranging from Thanksgiving to funerals and weddings. In most cases funds collected from these engagements were kept in a separate account. But those who played for a particular engagement would be compensated with a transportation token. The majority of the cash I earned from these engagements was what I used for lunch and basic school needs. Being a member of the school band, a chorister, and a scout placed me in an advantaged position for success in the sense that it earned me the respect of other students. Other students had special respect for those of us who engaged in such pursuits.

It is worth noting that in many of our engagements playing for the band, I was the main representative who would ensure that after we'd played, all instruments were safe and taken back to our band room. This was necessary after most engagements because almost every player, with few exceptions, drank alcohol. So most of the players ended up staying behind and having fun while I ensured that all instruments were safe and well stored. The reason I had been chosen was that I did not consume alcoholic drinks.

Many of my peers showed high respect for me and always consulted me for advice and suggestions, especially when it came to school issues. I was seen as a role model, and I was proud to support any of my peers who needed my advice. Sometimes I would even provide some of them with financial support so they could resolve some personal issues. I used my petty trading savings for this purpose. It was unlawful for students to bring goods to school for sale. If anyone needed to do that, it had to be done secretly and remain highly confidential. Sometimes I would take a few things in my bag to sell in class to get extra money to support myself financially.

School hours were from 8.30 to 3.30 p.m. from Monday to Friday. Exceptions to these hours were times when a student was required to conduct a laboratory test and needed to use the science room for that purpose. In such a case Saturdays were set aside so the student could come in and get the required training and support.

I had many friends at MBHS attached either to choir, the school band, or the scout movement. Most of my friends shared things in common, especially when it came to issues related to school or parents. We all had various challenges with either our parents or guardians. These challenges were usually related to discipline and compliance, both at school and at home. Some of the challenges almost all of us faced included making sure we helped with the housecleaning and ensuring we helped our parents. In most cases we tried to avoid doing housework.

Avoiding housework meant not going home early and then putting the blame on not being able to get transportation sooner. For me that was no excuse, though. My house was a twenty-minute walk from the school, so I usually walked to school and did not require transportation. I was no stranger to the responsibility of having to do housework. It was just part of my daily and weekly activities. In addition, I was solely responsible for housecleaning and packing. Interestingly, I did most of the cooking in the house for me and my aunty whom I stayed with at the time. Usually I would do most of my cooking over the weekends, preferably on Sundays, and sometimes on weeknights after school.

Usually when I planned the meals I was going to cook during the week, I would take the money with me to school so that after school it would be easier for me to take a pass through the market and buy all that was needed for my cooking. On one particular occasion, I took my market bag with me to school, and inside was the bottle I used to buy my palm oil for cooking. I actually made sure it was hidden well in my school bag so that none of my classmates would get a clue that it was in there. Unfortunately for me, one of my friends, who was also in the school band, wanted to put something in my bag and decided to go to my desk, collect the bag, and open it.

To his amazement he saw the palm oil bottle in the bag. He decided to remove it and place it right in front of the teacher's table for all my classmates to see. That became a cause for laughter for the rest of my classmates, to the point that they gave me the nickname of Palm Oil Bottle Boy. It was a serious embarrassment. It took me time to get over their provocation and taunts. What was certain was that I was focused and knew exactly what I wanted while jumping all those hurdles and enduring all that provocation. In fact, in many instances, some of those friends would accompany me to my house to relax and be fed food that I'd cooked. They all knew I was a good cook, and some of them wanted to learn and become like me—a good cook—but the opportunities were not there. All of those lessons and provocations helped to make me what I am today. They gave me strength and hope for the challenges that lay ahead. Today I am proud that those challenges gave me the opportunity to see life for what it is and accept what it brought and held for me and some of my classmates.

My experiences at MBHS were countless. I had a lot of great and interesting times. Also there were times when I did face difficult moments and challenges. I remember one particular point in time when I had a series of issues with my aunt whom I was residing with. She was a strict disciplinarian and an educationist. She wanted everything to be done perfectly. There was no room for mistakes. Many a time we both would have issues because I did not do the things she wanted me to do either at home or at school. I was convinced that what I did at home was right and figured that she would be happy with me eventually. But such was not the case. She wanted me to do things perfectly. Sometimes I was faced with these issues, and she and I would end up having some misunderstanding, which sometimes affected my ability to perform in school. But even with all of these problems, my high school days were the best.

I had both good and bad friends, and excellent teachers with a high sense of maturity who cared whether we succeeded in life. Many of my teachers in those days were strict but also friendly. They ensured we did things the right way and encouraged us to succeed with our studies. Failing to comply with rules and regulations was a serious crime punishable with a baker's dozen—thirteen hard strokes of the cane (a long small stick) directly administered to your buttocks. It was all fun. And there were the moments of pleasure when exams were finished and the results came out, with many of us having earned the required passing marks.

Discipline was the watchword for MBHS boys. You had to ensure you abided by what the principal and the teaching staff wanted. It was totally unacceptable for boys to do things contrary to school standards. For example, pupils had to be at the morning devotion. The dress code had to be strictly adhered to and could not be compromised. Finishing assignments and attending class was paramount. Failure to adhere to any of these standards made you liable for punishment by any of the top-ranking teachers responsible for discipline. A few at the time were responsible for discipline: Mr Levi Lewis, Raymond Pratt, and Mr Bodkin, all of them now deceased. When they punished you for mishaps and misbehaviour, you were sure from that point on never to repeat the same mistakes.

One of the things that struck me most, something I keep thinking about, is the manner in which teachers in those days handled pupils. They saw us as friends and pupils, but at the same time they played the role of parents and guardians. They were willing and determined to help any student who wanted to succeed with his studies. For those of us who were exceptionally serious and humble, they took a keen interest in us and provided all the support we needed to accomplish our dreams. How I wish that teachers of today would do the same and love the noble teaching profession. I am truly grateful and appreciative of all the support my teachers gave me and the confidence they instilled in me, and in some of my schoolmates and friends, to work hard and succeed in life. They were true heroes, leading by example. They were dedicated and committed to their jobs, even with the meagre salaries they earned. There is a powerful quote from Nelson Mandela: "Lead from the back and let others believe they are in front." In life it is important to trust and have faith in one another, especially when knowing that every human being on earth depends on other human beings. My school days were the best, but I can only be grateful because of my true friends and my dedicated and committed teachers. As the saying goes, school days are the best. This is truly a powerful slogan.

MBHS meant a lot to me. Knowing well the standards it upheld helped me to become the person I am today. Make no mistake, the person you will be tomorrow or today depends highly on those who influence your life while you're growing up. For me, my teachers and peers supported me in that way, and I am very grateful for them. If they were alive today, I would personally extend my appreciation for all they did in life. That is a fact. Remember always those you have interacted with, and appreciate them.

Sometimes it can be rough, difficult, and even disappointing. But one thing is for sure: you can always bounce back with self-determination and the support of those who help see you through. Therefore, never give up in any situation. The Bible teaches us to trust in the Lord always.

Chapter 4

Courtship and College Life

Having a family is a blessing when it is well-nurtured. It is God's intention that we should belong to a family and grow and become respectable individuals. My family life has undergone an interesting journey that I will share in this book. I started my family in my early twenties, when I eventually became convinced that my fiancée was the right person to get married to. This was interesting because it all started during our teenage years in secondary school.

I was in form three and my fiancée-to-be was in form two when we eventually met and started our courtship. The relationship itself started in church, as both of us were from the same church and were also in the Pathfinder club for youths at the time. The most interesting part of the relationship is that my fiancée was a twin, and her sister developed an attraction towards my best friend David in the same church. David and I attended the same school, MBHS, but he was a few grades ahead of me and also older.

As I was saying, my fiancée and I started our relationship. In no time we found ourselves doing youth visitation and belonging to the same group. So in essence it was easy for both of us to interact and discuss our outreach visits to other communities. This relationship and courtship lasted for almost seven years, and then we eventually decided to get married and legalize the relationship.

The first move to become engaged resulted in a big tussle with the family of my fiancée. The father of my fiancée was a policeman and was very strict in all ways. He is someone whom you cannot get close to or attempt to befriend. I and my friend David had a very good relationship with my fiancée's mother and her siblings, but not with our future father-in-law. We used many strategies and took many measures to try to build a good relationship with him, but all of that proved to be futile and fruitless. While we were taking all these steps to have one-on-one contact with our future father-in-law, arrangements were still ongoing to prepare for our respective engagements to the twins. It was an agreement between me and my friend and brother David that we would each get engaged to the twins on the same day.

Our relatives were informed and pleased about our desire to get engaged and be married. My parents and relatives were very supportive, as were David's parents. Initially, my mum believed that it was too early for me to get married and that I was too young, but eventually I persuaded her, and she agreed to support me. It was almost a year after I'd left high school, and I was waiting for an opportunity to enter university and pursue my law degree. David, on the other hand, had completed his high school some three years back and had been fortunate to get a job with a paint factory situated at the east end of Freetown. Fortunately, while I was waiting to enter university, I got my first job with Plan International after an intensive interview in front of a panel of six.

I was fortunate to go through the interview and was employed as an assistant social worker to be based in a community called Benguema, about three miles from my birthplace, Waterloo. I was doing very well with my work at Plan for almost a year and a half when I was suddenly approached by some missionaries who came to our church and insisted that they needed workers from the church to work in our mission hospital situated in the northern part of Sierra Leone some 160 miles from the capital, Freetown. While all of this was going on, I was busy saving part of my salary to apply for university to pursue my dream of taking a course in law and become a lawyer.

After the promotion by the missionaries, I and David, with another friend of ours now in the United Kingdom called Bankole, decided to move over to the mission hospital at Masanga in the north to work there. It was my first experience travelling away from the capital and going to stay with other people. It was an interesting experience when we eventually got to Masanga to start our mission work.

The entire environment was strange, and the village was completely remote with no electricity. The hospital itself was well-provided with all the basics and necessities, such as generated electricity for several hours during the day and a water supply coming from a well system. There was also table tennis and a volleyball court, where we spent all our evenings after work.

After working for almost two years at Masanga, David and I had the opportunity to be provided with scholarships to study outside Sierra Leone. Kenya was the country that was identified for our studies. It was David who was the first to start his course, and then I followed afterwards. It was during this period that we finally decided that we must make sure that the engagements were set before David's departure. Unfortunately, due to the urgency and nature of David's course, it was not possible to have all the arrangements finalized before his departure. About five months after David's departure, we agreed that the engagement should be done in his absence.

I was then the man in charge to ensure everything was finalized and that the engagement would go on. I did all that I could, being in constant communication with David and providing him with information on how things were unfolding. The fastest way of communication back then was through telephone calls, and those were very expensive. Anyway, I eventually succeeded in convincing the rest of the family members from my side and David's side. I received their blessings, and all arrangements were set. Our father-in-law-to-be was made to understand the reality of the event-to-be, and after several discussions and some persuasion, he agreed reluctantly. The engagement finally happened on a Sunday, with many of our friends and relatives present, together with church members.

Just a little more than a month after the ceremony, Florence travelled to Kenya and joined David. A little over five months after the wedding, I and Florella, my wife-to-be, travelled together to Kenya to join David and Florence. You can imagine the reunion with all four of us together in the same country. That day was a joyous one. David and Florence were at the airport to welcome us and pick us up.

The rest of the day was full of discussion and reminiscing of all that had happened over the last several months. My initial plans to become a lawyer did not materialize after I'd spent some months at Masanga working with vulnerable children and adults.

I came to the realization that social work was my calling and the best course for me to pursue. I eventually started my social work course at the Embu Development Institute, affiliated with Nairobi University. As I continued with my course, Florella and I were also making plans for how she could continue with a secretarial course which she had started back home. This was made possible by some of the savings that I had set aside while in Masanga and with some support from my sponsors.

As we all engaged in studies, the idea came up that we should have a wedding in Kenya at our Seventh-Day Adventist church in Nairobi. We started planning and involved several of our Sierra Leonean community members who were also present in Nairobi. We had lots of support, both financial and moral, from the Sierra Leonean community at the time. In fact, more support came from our godparents, who played a vital role in making all the arrangements. I would be remiss not to mention their names. They were Mr and Mrs Waretay, Rev Dr and Mrs Modupeh Taylor Pearce, Dr Ismael Peters, and Mr and Mrs Fred McCormack, the latter of whom is now deceased, bless her memory. These people were God-sent with strong family commitment and dedication. Their interaction and friendship with us led us to emulate their fine examples of love and true family friendship. They were committed to seeing us grow and form strong families of our own in the future. This demonstrated to us that many Sierra Leoneans are disciplined and loving and want to show love and care for others so that the latter succeed. That was exactly what our godparents demonstrated.

The wedding finally took place on Sunday, 15 July 1990, at the Nairobi Central Seventh-Day Adventist Church in Kenya. The wedding was the first of its kind. One of the popular Kenyan newspapers promoted the story as the wedding of the year, the reason being that David and Florence and I and Florella had gotten married on the same day—twin sisters getting married to two close friends on the same day. What an interesting moment. After the wedding we had a combined reception with toasts and speeches.

That was a moment of joy and was a dream come true. Florella and I had looked forward to that day for a long time, and finally it had come. Some things that happened on that day were very interesting. A Sierra Leonean elder who was our godfather recommended that David and I do our dressing at his house on our wedding day. David and I had awakened early in the morning from our usual rented boys' quarter to finish up the errands that needed to be done. We ended up at our godfather's house almost an hour before the wedding. In essence we had limited time to dress and be driven to the church. When we get to the house, our godfather was not there, but he had left all the instructions with his caretaker.

Once David and I got to the room and eventually went into the bathroom to take our baths, we realized that no water was available from any of the buckets in the house. We needed to at least take baths after we'd done all those errands. We decided to empty the toilet tank that was in the bathroom and use that small amount of water to bathe. You can figure out the kind of bathing that actually took place.

At least we managed to get through that. This just goes to show you how interesting things can turn out. But eventually with determination and God's blessing, you can succeed. And that was exactly what we found out for ourselves.

Florella and I ended our wedding ceremony that evening with happiness and joy and eventually returned to our small rented room. The next morning, I woke up very early to get a public bus that would take me back to my college, about four hours from Nairobi. I had to do that because I was to start my exams the next day, and I definitely needed to be present for those. One of my college friends had attended the wedding, so we both had to travel back to college. Some of my other classmates had not made it because of the exams. This was all planned. I knew I had a short time to ensure my studying was done.

I completed my diploma in social work with credit and eventually returned to Sierra Leone and continued my work with the Masanga Leprosy Hospital, as it was called at that time. I worked there for several years and then had the opportunity to take my master's course at Andrews University in Michigan, USA. Upon completion of that, I decided to complete my doctoral degree in philosophy as well. In all of these situations, I went through times of sadness and happiness. But above all it was determination on my part that helped me to succeed in my career path and become somebody useful who would contribute to my nation's development.

Chapter 5

My Christian Life

Serving God and becoming a Christian, and more so a Seventh-Day Adventist, was the best thing that ever happened to me. I wonder what I would have been or what my life would look like now if I hadn't converted and become a Seventh-Day Adventist (SDA) Christian. Thank God for letting me be one of his and for allowing me to serve him and others.

The Christian life is very interesting and inspiring if you have a relationship with our Creator. I grew up with my maternal grandparents in a village called Waterloo. Both my grandparents were Adventists, going to church on Saturday, the Sabbath as it was called. Since I was living with them, I, along with my three cousins and younger brother, who were also living with them, had no choice but to follow them to church every Sabbath. The Sabbath should not be violated by anyone. Everyone must ensure that the Sabbath is well kept to the letter. On Friday all purchases from the market were made. Before sunset we would have completed all the cooking to ensure that everyone could respect and observe the Sabbath. The Sabbath starts at sunset on Friday and continues until sunset the next day. The only cooking that is done on the Sabbath is the cooking of the foo-foo, a local food made out of cassava. Every other thing is cooked on Friday.

I always looked forward to spending the Sabbath with my cousins.

It was a day when everyone would dress well for church. In the evenings we had youth activities that engaged us in learning many things about the church and the Pathfinder youth movement. We did these things according to the commandment of the Bible in Exodus 20:8, which reads, "Remember the Sabbath Day, and keep it holy." This was an important factor in my grandparents' life, and I also followed that fine instruction from the Word of God, the Bible. Since that time it has remained with me to ensure that God's Sabbath is kept holy no matter what.

My father is a Methodist Christian and wanted me to be part of his faith and church. So periodically, my grandparents would allow me to attend Sunday worship at my father's church within the same village. Unfortunately, attending church service on Sunday was not pleasing to me, the reason being that nothing attracted me to the service. The Methodist church was unlike the SDA church. We had classes for young people and lots of activities that were aimed at getting you to like the church and its services. Eventually I and my brother decided not to attend the Methodist church anymore. This of course created some tension between us and our father, who wanted us to be seen attending his church almost every Sunday.

We persisted, and eventually he gave up. It is interesting to note that during those adolescent years, there were important Christian influences both at home and at church that shaped me, my brother, and my cousins into what we are today. Every aspect of our church activities was full of discipline, love, and care. That sent a strong signal to me. I realized that the church is a family that shares love and that is committed to helping and supporting one another. We grew up realizing that if we wanted to succeed, God should be first to direct and lead us in all we do. I grew up knowing that and trusting God to be my guide and protector for anything I do. I was encouraged to take my Bible seriously and read it frequently. So even though I was only a youth in the church, I decided to play a more active role. For me it was a blessing to belong to the SDA church and aspire to become a good Christian and set a good example for my peers and my community.

The SDA Church and the Sabbath is a command from God in the Bible found in Exodus 20:8, which says, "Remember the Sabbath Day and keep it holy." This command is given in the Bible by God himself and must be followed and obeyed. For me, reading the Bible and understanding the concept of the Sabbath actually changed my life completely. Even in my high school days, I took my church and my Sabbath worship seriously and tried to obey God and do what he wanted me to do. I truly believe that God's Word is precious and beautiful, and when we obey it, we have a great deal of joy and a peace that passes all others. I have seen a lot in my life, but this is the faith that has kept me going and moving forward, whether times were good or bad. I have never stopped doubting my God. Instead I thank him all the time for his goodness in my life and for seeing me through life's stormy moments, as well as through life's beautiful moments.

Christianity played a great role in my life and helped me become the person I am today. God is good all the time. I have never given up because I know that when it is the right time, he will always see me through. My Christian life is a testimony. It is what saw me through my school days and university period. Despite some of the hurdles I faced, God was in front, leading me through. It is impossible for me to think of doing anything as an individual or as a family without the involvement of God. I would definitely feel empty and guilty if I didn't involve God. I can testify that God alone has all the power to support us through all our problems and difficulties. I am a testimony of that, and I am never going to stop appreciating God and thanking him for who I am. Blessed be the name of the Lord. He has promised me and all those who trust in him that he will never leave us or forsake us. We only need to be faithful and steadfast in serving him. I have peace, and I have joy. For me nothing is too big or small when it comes to understanding the love he has for me and my family. God is good and will always be there for his children.

The difference between the SDA Church and other Christian churches is the Sabbath and the daily communion we have with our God. I have always trusted my God, and therefore I have seen all that he has done. God asks us to trust in him even when we walk through the valley of the shadow of death. He has given us the assurance that we need not fear anything. Why worry when you have a Saviour and God Supreme who will take care of you? I have sailed through life because of his promises. I encourage all who read this book to get closer to God and understand him well. And the only way this is possible is by reading your Bible closely and coming to know it well. Once you understand his Word and his teachings, brothers and sisters, believe me, your life will never be the same. Your behaviour and attitude will be changed, and you will come to appreciate God.

My whole life has changed because I have come to love and obey my God. I stand with strength and determination when things are rough and when the storm rages, but at the same time I stand strong and have peace believing that I have a God who is powerful. At the right time all will be well, and I will rejoice. I have seen it all with friends, with family members, with community members, with neighbours, with church members, and with workmates, but in the end victory has been mine when I trusted and believed that God is my only protector and shield. Never give up, but press on, and God will see you through as he does for everyone.

One consolation I have from being a Christian is that because of my faith and determination, I am steadfast and depend on God alone and nothing else. My Christian life has been a success story, not because of my own willpower but because of his faithfulness to me and my family. I say it has been a success, but this does not mean that I have not been faced with difficult and tough situations. I have been faced with these many times, and sometimes the situations I have faced have been terrible. But what has made the difference is having Christ in me and believing that any difficult situation will last only for a time and surely will pass. That is the difference, especially for Christians and even more so when one is a committed and dedicated member of the SDA Church.

Most people have failed in their Christian lives simply because they are confused and they look for quick, easy remedies. They are not committed to their faith. In addition, many of the Christians I have seen and observed depend way too much on their pastors and reverends to provide them with the Word of God. They don't read or research the Bible themselves. It is important to read and do research on your own. That is the only way we can understand the Bible and Word of God properly. Only when we succeed in reading and studying God's Word are we true to our conscience and believe what God wants us to do. Succeeding in life largely requires the intervention of God, especially for those of us who claim to be Christians. The Word of God promises us that he will never leave us or forsake us. God also tells us that if we trust and believe in him, he will provide for us and see us through. I have seen the goodness of God in my life and my family. Relying on God is the number one formula for how I came to be who I am today. I put God first, and then everything else comes to pass. The Bible itself says that when you put God first, he will also put you first. I have always appreciated being a Christian and being able to dedicate myself to God and others.

My family has trod the same path. My wife and children are all SDA members and are enjoying the benefits of being SDA Christians. Christianity plays a vital role in our family and provides the opportunity for us as a family to depend on and trust in our Lord regardless of what circumstances we are faced with. We know it's only through the faithfulness of God that we have been able to succeed as a family. I really want to thank God for making me who I am as a Seventh-Day Adventist Christian. It has made a difference serving my church, family, and community. To God be the glory. I admonish all those who read this book to get involved in the real and true Christian life.

The true Christian life is when you are really committed and dedicated to the things of God. Read your Bible and commit yourself to be steadfast regardless of the circumstances you are faced with, good or bad. Do not give up, but press on. You have to reach the realization, *Come what may, I am a child of God and will not deviate.* Once you are able to reach that stage through the power of God and the conviction of the Holy Spirit, nothing will be too big or too small for you. It certainly isn't in the eyes of our God. You will be filled with peace and happiness, the peace which passes all understanding, as mentioned in the Holy Bible.

Today many of our Christian brothers and sisters who profess to be Christians have failed simply because they rely on others to tell them what they want to hear. They don't read or find out for themselves. Many of our young people today depend on shortcuts, and many of them believe that when they become Christians, it is an opportunity for them to flourish and become successful in life. This is where most of them get it wrong. When you become a Christian and enter the church for a wrong reason, perhaps because you want to get married, get a visa, get school fees or an education, adopt a child, get a job, or meet whatever demands have been placed on you, you are doing the wrong thing. Then when you do not get what you entered the church hoping to receive, or when what you are hoping to have happen is delayed, you, like many of our so-called Christian brothers and sisters, leave the church or become a backslider because whatever intention you had for joining the church did not materialize.

A true converted Christian is one who will stay in the church regardless of success or difficult circumstances. Such a person will hold on until the day when God in his faithfulness follows through on his promise. That is the life I have experienced having a relationship with Christ. Nothing actually moves me. I have peace of mind, and I know my life will be long. God's promises never fail. It can take time before what he promises comes to pass, but at God's appointed time, whatever his plan is for each and every one of us will unfold, and then we will see the goodness of God, the King of Kings. I have been through many things in life with friends, church members, work colleagues, my community, and my university mates, but it has been only because of the courage and strength I received from God through my faith that I have endured. Be prepared to endure all when you are truly converted as a Christian. Seek his face and be prepared for anything that comes your way, believing that with God all things are possible.

There is a light at the end of the tunnel. Never compare yourself to others. God has plans for every human being on Planet Earth. It is left to each one of us to be sober-minded and continue trusting our good Lord until that day when we will see his face and enjoy his goodness. Remember that you can only be who you are, not anyone else. God loves us all and has made promises that will be fulfilled for each one of us. I believe this and have experienced it. That is why today I stand up, knowing that God is with me and my family in all circumstances. Just keep on climbing until you reach your goal. All things are possible when you trust and believe in God.

Chapter 6

My Family Life

Having a family is an enriching experience, one that I have cherished all throughout my life. I started my family soon after I got married to my wonderful and beautiful wife, Florella. She is simply the best and aspires daily to do what is right. It has been a blessing for me and for her that we came together to start a family. We have four wonderful and God-fearing children. The eldest is Sylvanus, twenty-six years old, followed by Marcus, twenty-three; Sia, nineteen; and Jessica, seventeen. All of them are doing very well, and God is blessing them each and every day. Sylvanus completed a degree in IT and software at the University of Greenwich, and he is back in Sierra Leone heading up his own consultancy. Marcus has just completed his professional course at the Manchester Football Academy. He aims to become a professional footballer. He is currently pursuing other professional courses in physical education and footballing. Sia is currently at the Washington Adventist University in Maryland, in the United States, pursuing biochemistry. Jessica recently graduated from Takoma Adventist College and is starting her university course in midwifery at the Washington Adventist University in Maryland, USA, the same university as Sia. It has been a blessing for me and my wife after bringing up children and having to take full responsibility for them. It is only through God's blessing that we have been able to do that. It is not because of chance, or our education, or what we know. It is only possible because we committed all our plans and activities to God's care.

Maintaining a family is a big challenge, but I can assure you that when you put your trust and hope in God, everything will work in your favour. God has promised us he will never leave us or forsake us. I trust in the Lord, as does my wife, and we pull together to support our children. We are proud of the direction they are taking. It is certain that God is their guide and protector.

We raised them up having them believe and understand that our home is a Christian home and that we believe in the Bible and nothing else. As they grew up, they came to understand that very well, and they too practised loving God and serving him. They are children who make a difference. They are role models and a blessing to the family and their peers. I remember when we relocated to the United Kingdom to ensure they got the best education as possible. That was a big, challenging decision that my wife and I took. We were doing very well in Sierra Leone in terms of God's provision and ensuring we stayed focused, but we also wanted to be sure that our children got the best in terms of education. We decided to relocate to the United Kingdom in 2009. That move meant a lot for us and our children.

As mentioned earlier, our children have been taught to respect their elders and everyone they come across. Relocating to the UK was a blessing for them. They were placed in different schools, and that is where a lot of things started to unfold for them in terms of challenges and having to meet and interact with different people from different cultures. For our children this was not strange. They quickly adapted to the system and the new culture. In church they were part of the children's class and youth activities. They were very respectful, sometimes to a fault. Many people around us in the UK admired them and sometimes asked lots of questions about their positive behaviour and friendliness.

In the UK our children quickly adjusted and made new friends. As a family we were always together, except for the few times when I had to travel and leave them on their own. But during those times I believed they were not alone because God is with them always. Life in the UK was full of lots of challenges, but as God's children, we found that those challenges helped us to press on and trust in God fully. It was because of those challenges that we became strong and realized who we are as human beings and what type of friendship we can offer to one another. My wife and I came to understand who our true friends were when we were faced with difficulties and challenges.

Of course we were not entirely strangers when moving to the UK. My wife and I had been travellers for quite a while, and the United Kingdom was one of our usual transit points in our many travels to the United States. We would stop over to see friends and other relatives. Before many of these journeys, friends and family members would encourage us to come over and join them in the UK. But as a family we knew exactly what was good for us, and we always worked towards those plans without being pressured by anyone. My wife and I knew that at God's appointed time we could stay wherever we chose to stay to ensure our children got the best education. So as we moved along, it was clear to us that the UK was the best option. And that was where God destined us to be.

And believe me, the whole process went smoothly except for one issue regarding the papers for Sia, our foster daughter. An approved work and school visa was not issued to Sia because the consul insisted that she was not our biological child. For us she was our child because she is part of the family and had been with us for several years. Not being able to get a visa for Sia was a devastating blow for the entire family. Many things rolled through the minds of my wife and me, questions like how Sia would be able to cope knowing she was not going to be part of this family anymore; what would happen if she had to stay with someone else other than the family she had known since age five; and how she would cope knowing that Jessica, her sister, was going to be leaving her and going somewhere else, not even a town in Sierra Leone but one outside the country. It was a challenge, and it left us struggling with what decision we were going to take.

As the head of the family, I discussed the matter with my wife, and we agreed that the first step was to pray and ask God for his direction, while at the same time we looked at the option to make an appeal. We had decided to keep the denial of the visa for Sia a secret between the two of us so that it would not become an issue for the children and so we could spare them the reaction to the news.

I worked on the papers again and had everything sorted out, and my wife and I did submit an appeal. After a week or so it came back with a second denial, but this time the visa was not the issue. So what was the next decision? Florella and I then decided that we would look for a solicitor in the UK to help us in filing another appeal for Sia's visa. We also decided that I would go ahead of the family to the UK to prepare the way and to start the filing process for Sia's visa.

I left Sierra Leone and arrived in the UK, where I started the process to search for housing and get a solicitor who would do the filing for Sia's papers. I got a lot of support from friends who were in the UK. They helped me out with getting the right house in the right area, taking into account security issues. My and Florella's idea was to mortgage a house, knowing well that this would help us in amassing some savings in the future. We had to secure the mortgage through a family friend residing in the UK. This was the easiest way to do it when I arrived. We were advised that it would be difficult to mortgage a house in our name since we had not spent any time in the UK. Anyway, we secured the house, and a close friend of ours introduced me to a practising lawyer in the UK who was Nigerian. I had several meetings with him, and we agreed on the cost. Eventually the documents were filled out and submitted.

After the documents were submitted, my wife and I decided to reveal what was happening to the children and let them know what was going on. We had to explain the situation to Sia, and we gave her the assurance that she would stay behind with my wife's sister-in-law until we got her papers finalized. According to the lawyer, it would be three months maximum for a decision to be reached on her application. The rest of the family would join me in the UK without Sia. This was hard for all of us, especially Jessica, who is Sia's best friend and closest sister.

When the rest of the family arrived in the United Kingdom, we paid serious attention to Sia's issues and dealt with them as our first priority. The lawyers requested that the other children each make a statement on behalf of Sia. The children agreed they would. In a few weeks, we received a letter from the lawyer informing us of the date to attend the court proceedings.

The day came when the court would hear the case. I remember all of us waking up that fateful morning, sending our supplications to God on the matter of Sia, and asking God to take control. We committed it all to God, and then we left the house for the court. It was in Central London that the court proceedings were going to be held. We arrived just a little after 8 a.m. The court proceedings were scheduled for 9.30 a.m. Just a little after 9.30 a.m., we were called into a small courtroom where a judge was seated. We entered with our lawyers, and the proceedings started. All the children were asked to leave the courtroom, and then they were called back in one by one to be interviewed by the judge. The lawyers started with the usual submission, with questions directed to me and my wife that needed to be answered. All went well, with everyone having their turn to answer to the judge.

After the proceedings we exited the courtroom and had a brief discussion with the lawyer who was presenting the case on our behalf. He told us that within three weeks we should get the final decision from the judge. He also mentioned that he was pleased with our answers to the questions and our responses to the judge and said that he had full confidence the case would be decided in Sia's favour. That evening we returned home with our hopes high, filled with the certainty that God would answer our prayers.

That evening we called Sia in Freetown to brief her on the proceedings. We encouraged her to pray, and we assured her that she needed to believe that all would be well and she would be joining us soon.

We started our hunt for schools, and we bought the basic stuff we needed for our newly found house in the UK. It was a complete change from what we had been used to in Freetown, Sierra Leone. We had to make a huge adjustment to the lifestyle in the United Kingdom. But with God we were certain that all would be well and we would succeed in what we were doing, especially at finding better schools and securing a better education for our children.

In a little over a month, we received the good news from our lawyer informing us he had received a letter from the court with approval for Sia's visa to be granted in Freetown. You can imagine the feeling of joy that everyone was filled with, especially Jessica. We quickly conveyed the news to Sia in Freetown and told her to start preparing herself to travel to the UK to join us. My wife and I agreed that I would have to travel to Freetown to collect her and travel with her.

Two weeks after that, I left the UK to travel to Freetown and collect Sia. I returned with Sia after a couple of days. It was a wonderful reunion with the other family members. From that day forth the family was complete, and we built a bond in order to work together as a family.

In the UK we started our new life, and because of God's faithfulness to us, we had smooth sail in settling in. We settled in very quickly, and everyone was occupied doing something. The children were going to school. My wife was undergoing nursing training to enable her to work as nursing assistant and earn extra funds to help run the household. It was not easy, but gradually we got used to the system, and we came to know so many things, both good and bad.

Our daily activities were scheduled, and everyone seemed to be programmed to do these things. We'd wake up in the morning and have our morning devotion. Then everyone would get ready for school or work. We'd see each other late in the evening or early in the morning of the next day. Life was full of many activities that needed to be accomplished as fast as possible. There was no time to be wasted. There was always something to be done. Everything moved very fast, but we kept trusting in the Lord, believing that it was just a matter of time before it would be over.

Our children were all making good progress in their schoolwork and doing well on their assignments. Because they were not used to the school system, we had to hire a private teacher to come to the house to assist them. As time progressed, they came to understand things very well and began earning high marks in class. They continued to perform well and made new friends in school and at church. Our family was blessed, and we had God's presence with us. Many of the unusual things that happened to us were part of the reason we were in the UK. We eventually came to see the reality of God's plan for us.

Our family's hope when we moved to the UK was that our children would get the best education possible so that in the future they could return to Sierra Leone to help the country and its vulnerable citizens. This was the intention and the plan. So the idea was to get everyone educated to university level and then allow them to make their individual decisions as to what was best for them. Unfortunately, these plans did not materialize in the way and manner in which Florella and I had hoped. But again we realized that God's plan was the best and that we should understand and accept it. It is not what we think is best for us. We can plan and choose to do what seems right to us, but we should also include God and allow him to make the final decisions.

Eventually our plans to stay on in the United Kingdom were thwarted when our final indefinite stay papers were rejected because some of the documentation was not available. I had to travel back to Sierra Leone after we'd finally submitted the documents the Home Office had requested.

At some point in this process I was requested to come to the Home Office for another interview. Unfortunately, my mother was sick with cancer and was at the point of death. I therefore chose to travel to see my mum, maybe for the last time, to provide assistance to her, being that I was the eldest in the family and I was the one who had to make most of the decisions. Fortunately, I travelled to see my mum, and we agreed that she would get further treatment in Ghana. She was in Ghana for almost three months and eventually returned to Sierra Leone. The treatment she received in Ghana, with the help of my younger brother and her sister aunty Rosa, both of whom accompanied her, allowed her to live for an additional two years. She finally passed away in January 2015.

Our papers were rejected when the Home Office realized that I had travelled to Sierra Leone. They could wait no longer to take a decision. We made several appeals, paying more than ten thousand pounds without any success, to get an approval for an indefinite stay in the UK. We actually needed the indefinite stay at that point for our children to be able to benefit from university scholarships and financial aid. Also they wanted to work jobs themselves and earn extra money to support their education. All these plans came to a standstill when our papers were denied four times in a row. Eventually, we prayed to God and asked for his direction. We came to the conclusion that we needed to return to Sierra Leone and think of what could be done next to help our children continue their schooling. At least Sylvanus, our eldest son, was able to complete his university studies after paying a huge sum of money as a private student.

We finally took the bold step and decided to sell our mortgaged house and some of our stuff and return to Sierra Leone. While all this was going on, I was already in Sierra Leone. At some point I wanted to return to support my wife and family and help them finish up and return, but again my visa was refused. The first time I was refused a visa to enter the UK, it was because my family was there and it was thought that my presence would cause them not to return to Sierra Leone. I actually said to myself that I wished the consul and those making the decision could know what was on our minds and what plans we had to return to Sierra Leone.

My family and I have always been hard-working people. We even made sure we saved some of our money for annual holidays. The only reason we were in the United Kingdom was to get our children educated. Then we'd return to our own country so I could continue with my humanitarian and social work. At no point did I think that I would settle permanently in any other country. I love my work as a development expert, and I love helping my country grow.

My determination always was to stay and support my country. So when my visa was rejected, it didn't hurt or make any difference to me. I only felt bad because I would not be present in the UK to help my family return home. Also I'd felt it was important that I be there to counsel my children about what had happened and tell them why we had to return to Sierra Leone.

For them the United Kingdom had over the course of time become their second home. We had stayed there for close to nine years. They had made friends and gotten used to the system. It wasn't long after our arrival that our children easily adjusted and settled in amid the culture of England. These were all the issues playing in my mind that triggered my reasons for going back to the UK. Unfortunately, I was not permitted to do so. I trusted that this was what God wanted. I concluded that I should just stay upright and allow him to act on our behalf.

Eventually, my family returned home, leaving behind Marcus, who still wanted to pursue his dreams as a footballer. He was staying in Manchester with my cousin because he was still in Manchester Academy and wanted to complete his studies. Marcus was trying to pursue other courses and find ways to accomplish his dreams. In the process of doing that, he came across a gentleman who was a sportsman who wanted to assist him. This man led Marcus to a footballing website that presented opportunities for young people who wanted to pursue their dreams in footballing. Marcus got in touch with the organization that operated the website and started communicating with two men, who apparently gave him the understanding that they were in charge of his case and application. He actually made some applications, and they provided him with all the associated funds.

Marcus was advised to pay the sum of 19,100 British pounds to purchase a full-time package to cover his visa application and his tuition and supplies for two years. He would stay in a boarding house and would then have the opportunity to join a particular team. Marcus informed us about this, and we too got in touch with the organization. We tried to negotiate a payment plan, which they accepted. I had to borrow money from family members and put that together with my savings to pay the full amount. It was during this time that Marcus had gone to his usual appointments at the Home Office in Manchester to report himself, as he'd been advised to do, because he was still in the process of getting his papers sorted out. On one particular day when he reported in, he was detained and asked to wait. We got in touch with him, and he told us that he was going to be in Scotland until further notice. We got in touch with the men who were in charge of the footballing association to inform them of the situation.

They got back to us saying they would now require full payment to sort out Marcus's immigration issues because things had reached this stage before Marcus could be removed from his detention in Scotland. I pleaded with them from Sierra Leone. We went back and forth, with me making expensive phone calls just to ensure that Marcus was safe and that the representatives of the football association would help him realize his dreams. Unfortunately, we could not arrive at any conclusion. Instead, the men said they needed the full amount before they would take any action. Believing that they were speaking the truth, having a website and a bank account with Barclays, we were all convinced that this was a true venture. I eventually paid the balance after going through an ordeal trying to secure all the money. We paid the full amount of 19,100 pounds.

After we made the payment, we expected the football association to help Marcus and get him out of detention to start his new course and enter the boarding house, as they had informed us would happen. Unfortunately, nothing happened. They came back with demands for more money before they would proceed. Eventually I got frustrated and was filled with stress about the entire process. I decided to ask them for a refund. At that point they told me the only way they would refund me was if I were to pay back some money. I went back and forth on the issue with them. To this day we still haven't gotten the refund. We had to hire a lawyer who assisted Marcus to get out. We eventually bought him a ticket to return to Sierra Leone so we could decide what to do next.

When I think of what happened, I am baffled and disappointed with the entire process. I really do not understand why of all places, the United Kingdom would allow people like this to register a football organization, give them a license to operate, and allow them to open a bank account just to defraud young people and parents who want to see their children achieve their dreams. To this day we remain in communication with this organization, pleading with them and telling them that the money we paid them was loaned to us so we could help our son achieve his dreams. I therefore make an appeal to anyone who might be connected to the British government to address issues of this nature and ensure such practices are stopped and action is taken against the offenders. Britain has a history of being honest and truthful with its citizens and with those who come to visit and do business. All these people need to be protected from such dishonest persons. I make this solemn appeal that Marcus's case be looked into and justice be done. The organization continues to exist. Its website is at www.professionalfootballersacademy.com. Marcus is still determined to realize his dreams, and we still support him to ensure that it happens. We need more people to support us and help him get justice. I appeal to the UK government, particularly the Home Office, to come to Marcus's rescue and provide him with justice. He still needs to pursue his dreams. It is our hope that he gets what he wants with your support.

God always has plans for his faithful. Our family's return to Sierra Leone was a large blessing. As a family we took on the challenge of deciding the next steps, especially for Jessica and Sia, who had become very used to the system in the UK and had made friends in school and at church. Now they had to leave all those friends and return to Sierra Leone, which they'd left almost ten years prior. But as God would have it, he didn't forsake his children. We decided that Jessica would relocate to the USA since she was a US citizen and that Sia would accompany her. At least the two of them would be together as sisters to continue their education and start university. Since Sia is not a US citizen, we had to apply for a student visa. We identified a university for Sia, the Washington Adventist University in Maryland. She was accepted and was given a spot to study biochemistry. All the plans were made, and the application was submitted for her visa processing.

She went for the visa on the scheduled day, and unfortunately the visa was not issued. It was sad news and a bad day for her and Jessica—and for the entire family. Given the relationship and bond that existed between the two of them, it would be difficult for them to separate. We thanked God all the same and deliberated a little on the issue. I personally interviewed Sia, asking questions about the interview, and she mentioned that the consul had not even looked at the documents or taken time to ask questions. The representative had only asked two questions and refused to look at the papers. All the documents Sia had at the time were valid and were good reason for her to be issued the visa.

Sia had even been given some funds for a scholarship to start at the university. Anyway, we started working on alternative plans for universities in Canada. As we were working on those plans, we also asked God for his direction. At some point God actually directed me to encourage Sia to make a second application to the embassy. At this point she had made contact with an Adventist university in Canada.

We decided to file a second application. We did so and were given a new date for an interview. When the morning of the interview arrived, we prayed and asked God to be with Sia when she went for her visa. She went in for the visa, and as God would have it, she got her student visa for the USA. She met a woman consul who was very warm and nice to her. The woman took time to go through the documents and ask Sia several questions. At the end of it all, she issued the visa. What a blessing. It was God's will; we needed only to trust in him. It was a big blessing to the family, and it taught us to understand fully that whatever we do as humans and as individuals, if it is not God's approved time for what we seek, it will never happen. God's time is the best, and when it comes, it truly blesses you and your family. We came to see that and to see God's plan for Sia and Jessica. Today Sia is at the Washington Adventist University pursuing her course in biochemistry. Jessica graduated from Takoma Adventist College and has been accepted at

Washington Adventist University to pursue her course in nursing. What a mighty and awesome God that we serve. God is good, and we must be faithful to him. I always believe and know that God has a plan for me and that I should continue to trust him and depend on him.

Who would have imagined it? Sia transformed herself from a young village girl who knew nothing about her future. God has blessed her to be someone who in the future is going to be a blessing to others. Sia has promised that when she finishes her course, she will help other village girls in Sierra Leone who need this kind of opportunity for a change in their lives. God works in a mysterious way to ensure his wonders are performed. God will continue to be with Sia and Jessica so that they too can be a blessing to other children who equally need to be supported.

My family life has been full of adventures and challenges that I and my wife have gone through. Above all it has been a blessing to have a family that is so sensitive to the things of God. That is the major thing that has continued to see us through. Make no mistake, without God and his blessing, nothing will work for you or your family. Sometimes things will work out and you will believe it is through your own strength or means, but believe me, it will fail very quickly if God is not present. My family life is based on the true principles of God, and this is what has made us into the family we are today. We are grateful for all his blessings. What more can we ask for?

My wife and I have four God-fearing children who are doing well. We have a house, cars, clothing, and much more, but above all we have Jesus, who is our guide and shield in all we do. Don't think that my family doesn't encounter problems. We do, but we always trust that those problems are challenges that sooner or later will turn out to bring us joy and happiness. For those reading this book, know that we as a family thank God for the little things that he has blessed us with and forget wondering about and thinking of those things we do not have. In his time, God will make possible for us those things we don't have. I thank God for our family, and I pray that God will continue to inspire us to bless others so that they too can enjoy a deeper family relationship with God.

Family is the backbone of a successful life if handled the right way. My experience has taught me that the husband, as the head of the household, needs to be sober-minded in the sense that he has to be focused and know exactly what he desires for his wife and children. The husband needs to be thinking ahead and ensure he does so in line with the other members of the family. It's also important to involve the children and let them provide their input into the household decision-making. The most important thing is that you put God first, trust that all your plans for your family are in his care, and know that he will unfold them at the right time. One thing I learnt and am certain of is that everything will not work out well just because you have faith and trust in God. It is not going to be like that. My family has gone through some difficult and terrible times—and I mean really tough times. When this happens, I wonder if there is any hope, and I start asking myself lots of questions.

In times like these, if I was not careful, my family would start playing the blame game, resulting in chaos. But one thing that is sure: I have never given up. I always throw those difficult moments back to God and ask for his guidance, also asking him to take control. In times like these, we pray more than before to ensure we stabilize as a family. But it is important to stay together regardless of the circumstances and believe that someday, no matter how long it takes, God will eventually see us through, as he has done many times.

Chapter 7

Friends

It is important to have friends, but also it is worthwhile to know the type of friends that you have. I have several friends, but in actual fact I can count on only a few of them to be real, true friends. Since my high school days, I have always cherished the idea of having friends. I had many friends while in high school, but not all of them were true, sincere friends. Some of them became my friends because of what they saw in me, and some probably because they wanted something from me. No sooner had they gotten what they wanted than they disappeared and didn't come back. I also made friends at my university, in my community, and at my place of work.

My attitude towards having friends entailed having an open mind and being sincere. I always wanted to make sure that my friends were happy, to the extent that I would sometimes make sacrifices to my own detriment just to ensure that the friendship continued and nothing hindered it. Many of the friends I made in school and university are still around, but I have little or no contact with them. Some of them have passed away, sad to say. But one thing that is sure is that I still have a few friends whom I do things with. The best of my friends are those I attend church with, although I have a few friends who do not belong to my faith.

As I struggled with coping with certain friends, I came to the realization that some people will seek to be close to you because of what they can get from you. So in some instances I had to ask myself questions about the sincerity of my friends because of the way they behaved. The reason I raise such questions is that these people behave poorly and do things that are unacceptable but then expect the friendship to continue. I have a lot of stories to tell when it comes to friendship and ensuring that it remains dignified. I have few friends I can count on and have trust in when it comes to many things. The bottom line is that I always seek to be frank and open with my friends, to the point that I feel obligated to do so even when it is clear they are not my true friends.

The simple reason I feel this way is based on mutual trust and love. I am the type of person who believes that I have to engage my trusted friends with issues and provide them with certain information, especially when I need advice or support for certain things that directly affect me or my family. I believe that whatever the circumstance, no man is an island and must not be seen doing things alone. I trust my friends and want to be open with them, believing that they too have trust in me when it comes to the things we do together. But sometimes this is not the case. In my experience, some friends are not open with me as I am with them. But in most cases, I end up being the one for whom good things unfold. It is not that I seek to find out the truth about my friends, but sometimes information just comes to me. And often I will give my friends the benefit of the doubt.

Allow me to relate some of my experiences of interacting with friends. As mentioned before, I have a few trusted friends within the church that I belong to, which is the Seventh-Day Adventist Church. I have come to realize that my church friends are mostly better off than those who do not belong to my church. It is easy to make friends, but the more difficult part is to retain those friendships. One friend I have had for almost decade is my friend and brother David Sombie. David is not just a friend; he is also a brother to me. We started way back, getting to know each other in high school and going to the same church. He is a real and trusted friend. The two of us have many things in common, and we ensure that we support each other. One of my other trusted friends and brothers is Alfred Campbell, whom I also met at church.

It is interesting to have good experiences together, but we must also be determined to support each other when the need arises. This is what I think friends are for, not to do things to the contrary. Friendship when handled well can yield many benefits for both parties.

Let me also state that friendship can be disastrous, especially when your friend is not a sincere or trustworthy person. I have seen it all and experienced it all when it comes to friendship. There are friends who only want to be assisted, and once they get what they want, they disappear. They will only come back when they have new problems that they think you are able to help them solve. It is therefore important that true friendship be demonstrated by both parties. I have been a victim of my own friends who have behaved in a distrustful manner and betrayed me on several occasions.

Some people will pretend to be trustworthy and open, but in the end they are exposed as the worst of friends. Some will even stab you in the back—your own friends whom you trusted! But as the saying goes, what goes around comes around. My experience has taught me many lessons about being very careful when dealing with friends. While having friends may be good for human beings, it is also important that you take time to discover whether your friends are true and honest. As I said earlier, it is sometimes very difficult to identify true and honest friends because of the manner in which some people behave. I found myself in a few situations where my own friends betrayed me. This is not unusual; it has been happening ever since history began. But one thing is clear—I have a clean conscience when I deal with my friends. I make no room for malice and jealousy.

The simple fact is that some people feel threatened because they either do not measure up or cannot be at ease with others because of their intent to destroy somebody else. Whatever the case may be, it is hard to understand why someone whom you refer to as a friend would want to destroy your reputation or cause you harm for no apparent reason. I have known these types of friends. In the end, what do they actually achieve by doing what they do? In most cases, they end up not succeeding in life because of their evil behaviour. For me, one thing is certain, and that is to continue trusting and believing in my God. It is important to note that when people plot against you, in almost every case they are the ones who end up in the pit. The Bible reads, "Though I walk through the valley of the shadow of death, I will fear no evil." God is with me all the time, and I have always seen his goodness and faithfulness. Eventually the evil practices of so-called friends are exposed.

When you meet new people whom you would like to be your friends, it is important that you study them well. Take your time to understand the essence of their friendship and determine if they are sincere. My experience with friendship has made me understand that the world is full of deception, jealousy, and hatred. Many people when they see you succeeding in life want to bring you down by all sort of means. They want to see that you become frustrated and unhappy. Be careful, because many of the front runners are usually those friends who are closest to you. As I evaluate my friendships, I realize that I have some sincere friends who, no matter what, will stand by me through any circumstance.

I believe that life must go on. Also I do not want to generalize, because there are still good people in the world who can be true friends for the purpose of sharing love and peace and thus providing the support that others need. I look for friends who are positive and who will make me and my family happy. My advice is not that you stop having friends, but that you evaluate potential friends and determine who will be a true friend. In life you need people, but you need good people, not bad people who will seek to destroy your life and leave you unhappy. You want to be happy and peaceful, so look for friends who will make you happy and give you peace of mind.

Chapter 8

Career and Employment

In this chapter I will take you through some of the interesting times I enjoyed while working for several organizations and also through some of the ugly things that I experienced. I have experienced quite a lot during my years of employment, for example the behaviour of staff, the way they do things, and sometimes the passivity with which they approach their roles and commitments. As an individual who has successfully completed my studies, I had a dream that someday I would be able to be employed and get a good job that would earn me a large enough salary to support my family. I always looked forward to the time when I would be employed and working with others. This was a moment I was hoping would come, and for sure it finally came.

I started my employment way back in 1987, when I had just completed my fifth form and was waiting for more opportunities to raise funds to start university. I wanted to work hard to earn some money for my schooling, so I had to start working very early. I worked for several organizations and experienced a lot at almost every one of the organizations that I worked for.

It is interesting to note the paradox that exists when you attend university or college and then eventually have a job and start working with others. Being part of the workforce is extremely different from the type of experience you have while in university or high school. In the workplace is where you start seeing the reality of life, the challenges that are ahead, and how you as an individual can overcome those challenges.

I found out that if you want to succeed in the workplace, then you must be tolerant but also very disciplined. If I hadn't been disciplined, many things could have gone wrong and I would have found myself up the creek. In any workplace there are many challenges. One of the greatest challenges is those who are jealous of others who are doing extremely well at work. I witnessed many occasions when staff pretended to be good friends or good colleagues, but deep within their hearts they held hatred for me. Sometimes I questioned why someone who was close to me would want to harm me or see my downfall.

For me this was one of the biggest challenges that I experienced when working with different colleagues. I had friends whom I helped bring on board at my workplace, knowing well that those whom you know and who are well qualified are likely to perform well. Unfortunately, I found out that a few of these people devised a way to betray me. So in essence, when you have friends and colleagues in the workplace, you need to be strong and understand that some of them are not truthful and can easily betray the cause of the organization if you are not careful. I have seen cases in which my closest colleague went all out to destroy my image and undermine my character.

It is important to know what type of friends you want to be with or interact with. Many of your friends and colleagues will respect you for the position of trust that you hold in society. The very moment that positon is taken away or the task is completed, many of these people will disappear into thin air and will never again come near you. I have experienced this in many of my jobs. I have held a certain position, and a lot of people would seek to be near to me. Some came for help, and some wanted to be around me because of what they stood to gain from me, but the moment I left that post or position, they fled and never returned.

I have found that many of the colleagues I interact with are hypocrites. They act in a manner that sends the signal that they support me and are ready to help, but the fact remains that they only want to get closer to me so they can find out how they can rob me of my title and position. They also want to get closer to me in order to exploit me. It's like they are agents of Satan, hoping to ensure that everything I do goes poorly or that I do not succeed. But because of my faith and beliefs, I am convinced that nothing bad is going to happen to me.

It is important that we all have an open mindset to stand strong to defend against all the challenges that come our way. Friends are valuable and helpful if we choose to have them. Some can be very supportive, and some can be very harmful and deceitful, especially those in the workplace. I have seen both these types of friends in my many years of work. There are excellent examples of friends I've had in the workplace who have supported me and strengthened me in times of difficulty. I've also had so-called friends in the workplace who would do anything to ensure I was victimized or frustrated so that I would leave and then they could in turn take over my job. I saw this sort of thing happen in different workplaces, and I always asked myself how someone could be happy seeing their friends at work being victimized or being blackmailed for no just reason.

I've tried to find answers, but I really don't understand the reasons or know what the answers are. However, I've come to the conclusion that many people who try to do things of that nature are not God fearing and have hearts full of hatred.

A workplace is meant for individuals to come together and share their talents to ensure that organizational goals and objectives are met. It is a place for friendship and family togetherness. A lot of employees spend nearly the entire day at the workplace. So given that we have to spend all that time in the workplace, why do some people choose to hate and do things that will hurt their colleagues? I find this practice bizarre and difficult to understand. Why do people want to undermine someone else's character? In the end, what does such a person gain? What does such an individual achieve by doing that? My experience is such that all those whom I've witnessed playing deceitful roles have ended up not even succeeding at getting what they'd anticipated receiving from doing what they did.

Others succeeded for a while, but at the end of the day their life's journey has never been favourable for them. In life we must understand that whatever we sow is what we will reap. If you sow seeds of friendship and kindness, that is what you will reap. If you decide to sow seeds of hatred and jealousy for no reason, you will reap the same, and life will never be successful for you or your family.

It is interesting to note that as I've travelled within and outside my country, I've continued to interact with colleagues with whom I've worked in various organizations or who have been my partners. Some of them are in very good leadership positions with respect and dignity, whereas others face numerous challenges just to survive, never mind showing leadership qualities. And in my evaluation, many of the successful ones who continue to be in leadership positions are those who stand for the truth and are upright in their business dealings. These colleagues are not hypocrites. They are true friends who have supported me and other colleagues without any form of betrayal.

Those whom I've come across who are struggling and trying to make a living are the very ones who attempted to destroy me and other colleagues in different workplaces. This actually illustrates the maxim that whatever a person sows is what he or she will reap. In life I believe that we exist for a cause. We should be each other's keepers, supporting and strengthening each other whether times are bad or good. That is the attitude that we as individuals should take to our various workplaces. The workplace is not meant to be a place where we fight each other and destroy other people's reputation and image. I have seen it many times where individuals whom you particularly trust and depend upon are the very ones who will frustrate you, destroy your character, and pretend to love and appreciate you, while deep down in their hearts they intend evil for you. I often tell my genuine friends and family members that I am afraid of no one but God our Maker.

If people think they should seek to destroy me or others, my good God will always fight for me and others who are true ambassadors of his will. What people need to know is that however long it may take, when they destroy others, they will surely be brought to justice someday and will suffer the consequences.

I am very thankful today for the faithful friends that I have. I am proud of those friends who have supported me in my struggles along my career path and who have been there for me in good times and bad times alike. One thing I've learnt from moving from job to job is that sometimes things happen in the workplace that we see as negative, but at the end of the day we realize that it was God's will for such things to happen. Everything happens for a reason. Almost every job change I made was an elevation from one level to the next. This is a clear manifestation that God, our Supreme Being, knows how to reward his faithful workers who are true to each other and their communities, especially those they serve.

Let me admonish all those who are blessed in the workplace and who have a profession to use your talents and gifts in the workplace to support other people so that the workplace will be like a second family home filled with love and peace. It doesn't help to victimize your colleague or friend in the workplace. What exactly will you achieve in the end? What benefit will you receive? You might succeed in getting something at the start, but watch out, because you will face justice in the end. The workplace is for professionals who should set an example for the rest of society.

If we cannot live up to the principles and values that our professions exemplify, then we are making a big mistake. Jealousy, hatred, and bad habits will destroy the image of the organization and slow the progress of the organizational objectives. Let us learn to solve issues by addressing them calmly when we are faced with confrontation by colleagues. If we practise this, then the workplace will be a better place where all will behave as family and trust each other.

Chapter 9

Travels

Travelling can be fascinating and exciting. It is always full of adventures and challenges. I have been privileged to travel to many countries in either an official or unofficial capacity. In both instances I have met lots of people around the world, different people with different talents and skills, people from all walks of life with integrity and dignity who are making a difference in the world by way of their professions. What is interesting is that in all of my interactions with these people, I have found that there is no great difference in terms of behaviour, culture, and values. Culture and values are interrelated in many of the places I have visited. There are lots of cultures and values that are cherished by countries and communities. But what is most peculiar is the fact that everyone in their own way cherishes their culture and tries to respect it.

The beauty about travelling, apart from meeting people, is that it is an opportunity to get to know many places and how these places express themselves to you as an individual and to outsiders. I have had the opportunity to visit several countries within the West Africa region. In comparing the achievements of the countries of this region, I am able to determine how such achievements would impact my own country. A simple example is Accra, Ghana, one of our neighbours not far from Sierra Leone. You see the tremendous developmental progress the Ghanaians have made within the space of a few years. Each time I've visited, I've seen that some positive changes have taken place to move the country further ahead. When I see all that, I always have lots of question in my mind about the future of my country, Sierra Leone.

I wonder what is happening with our leaders and in what direction they want to take our beloved country. I wonder why, what with all the travelling they have done to visit other countries in Africa, Europe, the USA, and Asia, they have still not taken adequate steps to provide the same services to our country's citizens. It's difficult to understand why Sierra Leonean government officials will travel to attend workshops and meetings in other countries, see the developmental progress made there, but then be so negligent about improving the country that we so love. It is my belief that they are just too interested in the personal gains that they get and are not invested in the best interests of our country. I wonder how on earth these leaders can be so selfish instead of putting their country first.

During many of my travels I have met many Sierra Leoneans who, as a result of the slow pace of the country's development process, have opted to stay where they are regardless of the difficulties and challenges they face. Sometimes I have tried to encourage them to return home and take part in the development process, as most of them are well-qualified professionals who could contribute a lot towards the advancement of our country. But again, looking at the way the country is moving in terms of development—at a very slow pace—no one in their right mind would want to sacrifice their current job to return, only to find that there is no opportunity for them to contribute positively. I've discovered that most of these people prefer to stay where they are and wait for the time when things can improve. This is what everyone hopes for. I know many people who have waited for a very long time and then finally passed away hoping that things would one day get better.

The matter greatly relies on our leaders to be more disciplined and show patriotism for our country. We all need to put the country first in all that we do and also ensure we do the right thing. Many of our colleagues do not have an interest in making sure the country develops. They are only interested in themselves and how they can be corrupted or engage in corrupt practices to get rich overnight. And the truth is, many of them do so without any regret. May God have mercy.

Travelling over the years has been great fun. Travel changes your perception of so many issues, and you learn how to appreciate people and what they do. One of the most interesting things to me when I travel is the cultures that countries practise. Every country I've visited has its own way of doing things. They all cherish their culture and ensure that everyone is part of it. Some of the cultures sometimes give me culture shock, especially when I think of my own culture and how we do things. I see these things in other cultures done differently. I wonder how the people cope practising some of these cultural traditions.

For example, I studied and lived in Kenya for some years. In Kenya, when you visit a family's home, the first thing they will do is offer you a glass of water. Also their eating habits are different from what we have in Sierra Leone. In Sierra Leone we have rice as our staple food, whereas in Kenya they eat more of potatoes and meat. I had the opportunity to travel to Thailand in Asia, and many things the people do there are quite different from our practices in Sierra Leone. The way they dress is different, as is their language and food. The good thing is that many other things I have seen while travelling are things that we share in common, such as having respect for elders, having a family, and having a good attitude towards one another. At the end of the day, we see ourselves as one people but with different cultures.

I made lots of friends during my travels, and I realized that all of these people from different countries demonstrate different character in their own ways. This is either because of their culture or the result of the country they came from. What is interesting is that every one of the people I have met all have their own unique ways of doing things and of associating with me and other people. Sometimes it is the way they talk, the way they smile, the food they eat, or the interaction and the experiences they share. I have found out that even though we are from different countries, we are all the same as people. It is good to see that we have similar cultures and behaviours. I have found this to be unique in terms of who we are and what we mean to each other.

The one thing that struck me the most is that whereas I've met new people, made friends with them, and shared experiences with them, in the end I had to part with them. Sometimes, depending on the relationship, some of the people I crossed paths with left deep impressions on me. Some, of course, I have formed long-term relationships with. We continue to exchange emails and phone calls. Others I've met I knew for just that particular time period, and the only thing I think about is the special moments I shared with them either in a workshop or while on some adventure visiting some tourist areas in the countries I visited.

Travelling is part of me and one of my hobbies. I like travelling, meeting people, discovering new places, and getting to expand my knowledge of other cultures, other people, and other countries. In my extensive travels, I have always asked myself, *Why would Sierra Leone not emulate and practise some of the good qualities demonstrated by many of these countries?* Even some countries in our own neighbourhood have these good qualities. So what is it that our government officials do when they attend meetings and conferences abroad? Do they come back to report on those things or try to put the things they have learnt into practice? It's difficult for me to understand how officials travel on behalf of the country and yet refuse to implement simple but important things that would benefit the country and ensure that we too are a light to our counterpart countries.

When I travel, I see the many good things that these government officials also see, but nothing is done to emulate and practise the good things so that Sierra Leone too can succeed and develop. Instead we continue to deteriorate and fail to move forward. I believe that many of our government officials do not like our country or its people. They are just bent on spending the resources we have for their own selfish purposes and not putting any effort into ensuring the country develops. Officials in leadership positions should be asking themselves these questions:

- What is it that I have done during my tenure that has changed my country and helped make it develop?
- What one or two unique things have I instituted that others will come and say that this was my work?
- Is my conscience clean that during my office term I have done the best I was able to do to ensure that the country would develop and grow?

We citizens, those of us who serve the people, also need to be asking ourselves these pertinent questions.

One of the greatest legends and leaders, Nelson Mandela, said, "Lead from the back and let others believe they are in front." What a powerful statement. Sometimes when I travel I am saddened for my country and wish that I had all the power in my hand to change the entire picture. For me travelling is an opportunity to see the world and use the best things I find there to change my family, community, and country. I would like to admonish all our leaders who have the opportunity to read this book to be true to their conscience when they serve their people.

It is important that our people trust our leaders and depend on them to change their lives. In Sierra Leone, many of our people have lost hope in our leaders, as they continue to fail us and lie to us. Corruption is at its peak, and you ask yourself why one man would want to acquire all the wealth when thousands of disadvantage people are suffering. Don't these leaders have a conscience? Don't they understand that if you sow bad seeds, you will reap a bad harvest?

I plead with our leaders to change their attitudes and have love for Sierra Leone and all the leaders of other countries. Our people are looking up to us to change their destiny. We have to be true to our conscience and realize that God sees everything that we do. Don't accumulate wealth at the expense of the very people you serve. If you do that, be assured that it will not yield good fruits. Even your own generation will be cursed. As we continue to travel, let us use it as an opportunity to learn from others so that we can come back to our country and implement those things which will develop our country.

Today in the twenty-first century, what many people must do before leaving their home country to travel elsewhere, say, to Europe or the USA, to look for greener pastures and just to survive has changed completely. Today, I don't need to travel elsewhere to succeed in life. The opportunity can be found and the goal can be achieved if our leaders would only create an enabling society for us where inequality is avoided. Our leaders need to ensure that we have the finest opportunities to do things on our own and become a nation of people who will live in peace and succeed in life. We need equal opportunities for everyone, including girls and young women, so that peace and tranquillity can prevail.

Some years back I had to relocate to Britain to ensure that my children got the best education. Education is a priority for every country, something that must be developed. Over the years in Sierra Leone, education has deteriorated to the point that many of our students who have graduated from our universities have a hard time coping in the workplace. Many don't even know how to use the computer. It is sad that our leaders have not paid attention to these all-important issues. I am hoping and praying that facilities will be created so that our people no longer will have to leave this beautiful country and migrate elsewhere just because our government and leaders have failed to provide basic opportunities needed for children and youths who tomorrow will be the leaders of our country. Sad to say, I have yet to see our leaders be true to their conscience to ensure that opportunities are created for every sector to succeed. Sierra Leoneans cannot continue to suffer and find it necessary to travel outside their own country in the name of searching for greener pastures. Our country can make all of those needs available if only our leaders would be sincere and true when it comes to national development.

Chapter 10

Living Abroad

My family and I had the opportunity to live abroad in several countries. Those were exciting but challenging times. My wife and I lived in the United States, Maryland to be precise, to work and study. It was during our early years, when we had young children, that we moved to the United States. It was in the year 1996. We had two sons. Sylvanus was barely six years old, and Marcus was a little over one year old. So we were a family of four at the time. During this period, I was working for a church organization called Adventist Development and Relief Agency (ADRA). I was the associate country director at the time.

The opportunity came when I had to undergo a hectic process to gain entrance for an internship at our head office in Washington, DC. The internship was meant to train young professionals who had been with the organization for some time. It was a tedious process. The programme itself required four people in total, and the invitation to apply was sent worldwide to all 130 countries where ADRA was operational.

At the end of the six-week process, I turned out to be one of those who was chosen for the internship. The package included a one-year intensive programme of activities that were to be conducted at our headquarters in the United States. I took my entire family. That was a big blessing, and I still ask myself how it all came to be. I was later made to understand that there were more than two hundred applications at the time, but God was so good to ensure that I was among those who were chosen.

After I'd received the letter by fax informing me of my success, the next step was to start making travel preparations and get all the documentation together for my visa. My boss at the time was happy for me but also cautioned me that it was one thing to get the internship scholarship and another thing to get the visa. I answered him that it was a definite possibility that I'd get the visa. I assured him that God, who had allowed me to go through the whole process, would see me through to get the visa.

The day came when I was to show up for the visa. I had completed all the required paperwork for myself and the rest of my family. I showed up with the rest of my family that morning at the US Embassy at seven o'clock. The office was jam-packed with people, all of whom had shown up for visas. The embassy at the time was located right at the city centre adjacent the capital. It had the famous cotton tree mark, the symbol of the capital city. There was a long queue of people outside, all waiting to be called inside. Around 8 a.m. we were provided with numbers and ushered into the waiting room. The room was fully air-conditioned. There were chairs facing a sealed transparent glass window that had about four openings where interviews were conducted. Interviews started around 8.45 a.m. Names were called, and the people were asked to move forward to one of the interview windows. At the interview window questions were asked, and you were required to respond. Those of us seated facing the interview windows listened carefully as questions were asked. The room was tense and quiet as each individual waited for his or her name to be called. My turn eventually came.

I was called upon to present my documents. I presented my documents and those for my family as well. The consular was a tall slim woman with small eyes and long greyish hair. She was dressed in a light blue blouse and had a cup of tea on her desk. She welcomed me and greeted me with a gentle tone voice and asked me how I was doing. I responded in the affirmative and said, "I am fine, thank you." At this time she was going through the documents page after page while at the same time looking at me and my children, who were age six and age seven months at the time. She asked several questions, among which was what I would be doing if I were permitted to travel to the USA. I knew exactly what I was going for, an internship for a work-related programme that had to do with my current job. I told her that all expenses and related costs would be covered by my international office.

She moved on with the process, looking at the documents. At one point she pursed her lips, carefully looked at me, and said, "Sir, your documents are fine and your responses seem convincing, but I am afraid I can issue the visa for you only and not for your children or spouse."

In a low tone and a respectful manner, I said to her, "Madam, it doesn't make sense to give me a visa but not give one for the rest of my family. My kids are very young, and they need to have my attention as a father. I can't afford to leave them behind, especially for such a long period of time." We discussed the matter, going back and forth for several minutes, after which she was convinced that she needed to issue visas for my family as well. She suddenly became very friendly and even requested other, nicer photos of our children than those we had submitted. In the end, the visa was issued to all of us. I was very grateful and thankful to God for answering my prayers. A few weeks after that, we had to sell most of our belongings and then travel to the USA.

Arriving in the USA presented us with an opportunity to see the great nation that everyone spoke about. The wealth, the scenery, the beauty, the buildings, the roads, the houses, the green fields—it was beyond comprehension. It was amazing to be in the USA and to have the opportunity to start my internship with three of my colleagues. They were from Ghana, Ethiopia, and Peru. We started our internship and got to learn a lot of things, especially the food security programmes that ADRA was implementing in several countries with the support of USAID. It was an excellent experience from which I learnt a lot. I also had the chance to travel to some of the implementing countries, like Bolivia and Thailand.

As a family we had a nice two-bedroom apartment that was

fully furnished and rented by the office, with a monthly stipend for me and my family to take care of our living expenses. It was quite fascinating to see how things were different to us, coming all the way from Sierra Leone. But we learnt several important lessons about life while in the US.

My wife and I came to appreciate what we had left behind in Sierra Leone. Of course in some ways Sierra Leone can never be compared with the US, but in terms of other things, it is far better when it comes to friendship, love, and community togetherness. We realized that the fabric of society, the norms and culture that binds people in my country together, was missing in the United States. The longer we stayed, the more my wife found it difficult to appreciate US culture, her having to stay home alone with the kids and just watch TV and do nothing else except read when possible.

The friendships and the church and community relationships we were familiar with in Sierra Leone were absent in the United States. This started causing a lot of problems for my wife. I had the opportunity to travel a great deal and had to leave my family behind when I did so. This of course did not help my wife's situation. If and when possible, she had a few phone conversations with some of our closest friends, who in many instances were busy with work and did not have time for interaction.

Not too long after the internship ended, I was asked to move to Ghana to work for several months with our ADRA office there. In Ghana the situation changed quite a lot in terms of our being lonesome and bored at home. We made lots of friends and came across many Sierra Leoneans with whom we shared friendship and love. The church was also encouraging, and we had a lot of things in common with the Ghanaian culture. So life in Ghana was much better in terms of being able to move about and do things our own way. In Ghana I had the opportunity to work with several people and also to make many friends. Ghana was fun. We finally left with many fond memories. At least our life in Ghana was more peaceful and gave us less stress. A lot of things happened there, and we thank God for that.

After almost a year in Ghana, we moved back to Sierra Leone. I eventually became the country director for ADRA in Sierra Leone. A few years after that, I resigned, having worked with ADRA for almost twelve years in various locations. I left and started working with Right to Play as country manager, a post I held for few years. It was during this time that I and my wife agreed that for the sake of getting our children focused and stopping all this travelling, it would be nice to settle for a while and get them a proper education. We eventually came to the decision to relocate to the United Kingdom to ensure that our children got a better education that would see them through life. For me it was important that our children get the best education to ensure that they would sail through life with fewer difficulties and challenges than I had faced. We eventually started the preparations, and in June 2009 we relocated to the United Kingdom.

Arriving in the United Kingdom was also a challenge because it required making adjustments and becoming familiar with the systems of the UK. While it was a challenge, we were also banking on friends who had lived in the UK for a long time to provide valuable support to our family as we were settling in. No doubt, we received tremendous support from a few friends. It was not an easy task to get everything finalized. We had to look for housing for our family and for schools for our children, and I and my wife both had to find jobs. We managed to get all of that settled in less than four months, for which we thank God and our reliable friends.

We started off very well, making sure that all that needed to be done was achieved, especially finding the right schools for our children, getting our UK driver's licenses, and finding jobs. All of that fell into place as we strived to settle down. During the process of settling down, I experienced many things as an individual, and we experienced many things as a family, that I definitely would like to include in my book. One thing I discovered is that you cannot afford to settle down without having friends or family members to help you out, especially if you have never lived in the UK before.

I found out that you need at least some resources because no one, not even your close friends or relatives, will provide you with the required funds to start out. One good thing was that my wife and I had savings and service benefits that we could rely on in the process of settling down. I also realized that people will provide you with support when they see and sense that you are not going to be dependent on them. Otherwise the support you get is not going to be tangible. Thank God in my case that our friends and family members realized that we were not going to be dependent on anyone, so they were willing to support us. This was because they knew that we were not going to be a burden to them. That was one good lesson for me from the start. It motivated me to be more serious about managing my resources well.

Our staying and living in the UK was rife with lots of personal and family issues which, if it hadn't been for God's blessing and our hard work, would have derailed our entire purpose and aim for relocating to the UK. I give thanks to the few friends who stood firm and strong to defend and protect us when we were faced with numerous challenges. I came to understand that it is when you have real problems that you know who your true friends are. We faced some challenges, the overcoming of which was crucial for our continued stay, and for all of these things, funds and resources were needed. It was only by God's blessing that we sailed through those processes. The support will be there from friends who you know at least will support you, but in the end this was not possible for us. People we had known for only a few weeks or months were the ones who surprised me and my family by providing the support we needed.

I came to understand that in life not all those who smile, laugh, and play with you are your true friends, your true brothers and sisters. God may send people who are true friends, true brothers, and true sisters to rescue you when you are in difficult circumstances. I saw this happen, and I learnt my lesson and came to trust that in the midst of all these challenges, we still had many individuals who were sincere in their friendship and association with colleagues and others. I also learnt that bad experiences suffered must not deter me or others from doing what we can to help others. People can behave the way they behave, but that should not change what we believe, and that is to be truthful to our conscience when we have friends and outsiders who support us during difficult times, friends who will not run away or even seek to destroy us when we are faced with a situation of this type.

Gradually I understood what it means to relocate to a foreign country and to stand the test of time. With all that I've experienced, I look at my past and my professional life in Sierra Leone and compare it to my life in the United Kingdom. I see a vast difference in terms of the various levels of problems that I and my family encountered. As mentioned before, the only reason for our relocation was to get a better education for our children. That was it, nothing else. So looking back at my life working in Sierra Leone after returning from my studies overseas, I realize that life in Sierra Leone is far better, all things considered. Ever since I returned home from my studies, I enjoyed every one of my jobs working as a development professional.

These are the reasons why I concluded that life for me was better in my country. I preferred to live there rather than relocating to the United Kingdom. In my country I have the opportunity to mingle with and help disadvantaged people, especially young persons and children who are disadvantaged. I get a special feeling of joy and peace knowing that I have contributed to the safety of my fellow Sierra Leoneans and improved their lives. I also have time for my family and children.

Even though my job was of high profile and included difficult tasks, I still had time for my family and community-related activities. Above all, my income and doing other small related jobs was just enough for me to be able to keep my family going. I could even use part of my salary to assist others.

Relocating to London changed my life completely. I realized that many of the things which seemed to be easy for me to do in my country were hard and challenging there. Firstly, trying to get a job, even as a professional, was a daunting task. It took me several weeks to be able to get a job related to my field. I also noticed that there was not enough time for the family since I and my wife were out almost all day and sometimes late into the night. Everything changed completely. We had to make a lot of adjustments to ensure we succeeded both in our home life and our social life. At least our children were grown-ups, so they needed very little supervision.

I remember when we were about to relocate. Many of our family members and friends had this feeling that life in London was going to be better for us, especially when it came to making more money and increasing our income base. Unfortunately, this was not the reality. For me it was even worse in London. I found it more difficult trying to cope with the income that I and my wife earned each month. When we had finished paying all the bills and taxes, we were left with nothing and had to rely on savings from working for years back in Africa that we had kept for our children. The income that we earned in our home country may not have been as much as we earned in the UK, but the expenses in the UK were huge and plenteous, unlike in our home country.

In Sierra Leone I didn't have to pay rent for a house, whereas in the UK this was something we had to do. The bills were simply incredible. The situation is such that you are not at peace with yourself. There is lot of stress and tension almost all the time and sometimes even frustrations. The benefit, though, was that our children were studying hard and getting a first-class education. That in itself cannot be compared to the sacrifices we had to make. So in essence we were getting a better and more valuable education for our children in exchange for losing the comforts that we used to enjoy back home.

It was the same for many of our friends who had lived in the UK for many years. For many, life still continues to be a challenge. Survival for them and their families seems impossible because of bills, family commitments back home, and other financial commitments that are paramount and that need to be sorted out every month. Many of them have lived in London for many years but still have serious challenges when it comes to coping with the system. For many the benefits are that at least their children are attending good schools and getting a better education. But also it's about ensuring that what they earn at the end of the month can meet all their needs. At the end of the day it is certain that for many people this is not the case.

Most of the parents end up having two jobs or working extra hours just to make ends meet. When this is the case, the children suffer from not having the parental care they need. Most of these children make friends who are a bad influence on them, convincing them to take drugs and become socially defiant.

So at the end of the day most parents end up having many problems with their children because they have no time to supervise them. What is true, though, is that the United Kingdom offers many opportunities for families and students to strive to become successful in life. There are opportunities in the area of education, there is good healthcare offered to those who have valid work permits and visas, and there are opportunities to earn extra income if you are a hard-working, committed individual. Above all there are opportunities to rapidly change your life if you are an individual or family who is serious and does not make too many unwanted demands.

On the other hand, those who are not eligible for valid work permits and a better education in most cases find it difficult to survive and complete a course of study. I look at some of my colleagues who have lived in the UK for a long time and wonder at what point they will determine to return to their home country to help in the development process. There are thousands of Sierra Leoneans in the UK and elsewhere with various professional qualifications who could make a great difference if they were to choose to return to their home country. The impact would be huge and extraordinary if these qualified people would return home.

Even their children I wonder about. Many of these children were born in the UK and have developed within that culture and have come to accept it. So you realize that in the future those children will be helping to build up the UK rather than building up their country of origin. We will continue to experience a great brain drain and will have fewer qualified people to support Sierra Leone in its development. Many of these children have not even visited Sierra Leone, and therefore it would be hard for them to "return home" or to help in developing the nation. So in essence, when a family moves overseas and raises their children in that particular culture, their children will grow up amid that culture, and thus the conviction of many of them after completing university will be to stay in that particular country and settle down. When I look at the issues and problems we have in my country and many other African countries, I see that they stem from this problem. Many of our African brothers and sisters who have become successful over the years find it difficult to return home and help in nation-building.

In some ways, we cannot really blame them, the main reason being that many of them were born and raised in those countries and have never even had the opportunity to visit their mother country or develop some interest in it. Another reason is that some of the families after relocating feel strongly that they are not even African. Rather, they feel they are citizens of the country in which they have become naturalized.

All of these factors are reasons why my country continues to lag behind. I have witnessed that others who have naturalized have demonstrated their patriotism by giving their full support to the country to which they currently belong. They have periodically encouraged their children to visit the country where they were born before relocating to wherever they now find themselves.

In some instances, I have also witnessed that some of these children don't even want to hear about the African country where their parents come from. They regard themselves fully as nationals of the country in which they were born and want to have nothing to do with their country of origin. It is really sad that this is happening. I wonder when the realization will come for things to get better. Living abroad has increased my thinking and helped me to understand very well what life is all about. For many, relocating abroad means changing their lives so that they can make a quick buck and enjoy the rest of their lives. For others, relocating means trying to get a better education and find greater opportunities so that they can become successful individuals and in the end return to their home country and help in its development process. Others relocate for various other reasons, including wanting to travel overseas because they see others returning home with all sorts of false information about the good life and making quick money. Some want the adventure and think that maybe somehow life will change by way of mere luck, or perhaps they will get to know someone whom they will end up marrying. At the end of the day, most of these people forget about the many numerous challenges that they will have to overcome in order to survive and be successful.

Today we see that many of our brothers and sisters who have travelled abroad are facing serious challenges trying to adapt to the systems in which they find themselves. What they presumed was the good life has ended up being a civilized form of modern slavery in which life itself has no meaning. So you ask yourself why many people want to venture out when most of them know the risks and difficulties associated with doing so. Many of my own countrymen, even with a master's degree and a doctorate, are facing serious difficulties trying to survive as individuals and as families.

When I assess my own situation living in Britain, many realizations come to mind. I always ask myself why I would want to stay in a country with millions of professionals where my input and professionalism counts for little, provided it is even seen. Why not, with all my education, return to my country and help in nation-building rather than struggle to get the right type of job that will enhance my career path? I think of the jobs I used to have and the high-profile senior positions I held at organizations that helped society. I think of all the impacts I made and the communities that I supported, changing the lives of many children, youths, and women. I know the joy and happiness that come when I see the tremendous transformation in the lives of many of these people. For me it was a blessing to serve and help those individuals, as it is a blessing to help my country develop. I saw the prospect of staying in the UK as a waste of time in the sense that I had a task at hand to reach out to those who were disadvantaged and in need support.

Make no mistake, going to the UK can mean a lot and can change your life when you have a goal and the ambition to develop yourself and acquire better skills and knowledge. You get those skills and make use of them when you are privileged to serve and support your home country. If only we had more colleagues with a vision to support their home country, then our country, and many other African countries, would develop rapidly. And when that happens, Africa will be a better place for everyone to live and settle down.

It is important therefore to evaluate all the various reasons when you think of settling abroad. Don't get me wrong, I am not saying that settling abroad is good. But what is your motive for settling abroad? Is it for getting a better education and skills, or are you looking for greener pastures, as many say? For me it was about ensuring that my kids were well educated so that they would have the best opportunities once they returned to their home country to help in nation-building. But that is not all. I spent a great deal of time helping them to understand where they came from and making sure they liked their home country.

I also introduced them to many of the issues of Sierra Leone so that in the future they too could pay back by helping disadvantaged people. So that was the main reason why I and my family relocated to the UK. It was surprising to see many other Africans who lived in the United Kingdom and many other countries with no sense of direction. They only lived day-to-day with meagre jobs and had no determination even to educate themselves so that they could become more productive for themselves and their home country. It was difficult for me to understand why some of those people lived amid such circumstances that caused stress and frustration. I spoke with a few of them. After hearing their stories, I decided that if it were me, no matter what the situation was, I would rather pack my belongings, if any, and return to my home country. When I advised some of these people to take the drastic decision to relocate home, they came up with lots of excuses that actually made no sense.

For me I see all the benefits of coming back to my home country. I see the opportunities to continue serving the people who need me most and not serving outside my country, where I was not needed and not even recognized. I came back and made a great impact by changing people's lives. I have a sense of peace and joy when travelling within my country to hard-to-reach areas, seeing the suffering people and providing what little support I can to change their lives. That in itself is worth thousands of blessings. I'd rather do that than waste my time looking for money overseas that I know I will never get, not even in my dreams. I prefer working with my own people and realizing the joy and happiness they experience when their children are helped going to school or provided with medical support and clean water in their communities.

One positive thing I experienced while living abroad was having the determination to study, learn skills, and gain knowledge. The fact that I stayed in the UK and came to understand the culture provided me with the discipline to do things which are morally right. My overseas experience taught me to be disciplined in all ways. So when I returned home, I had the discipline to do things right. I did not allow others to influence me wrongly; rather, I was determined to positively influence those I worked with in many ways, ranging from not being corrupt, to treating others equally, to ensuring that everyone is provided with the opportunities that they should get, to refraining from supressing colleagues and pulling them down, which is one of the most rampant forms of destruction in our society. To me it makes a lot of sense that our colleagues who have studied abroad and acquired discipline should use that to influence people at home. If that were to happen, a lot of changes would occur.

Living abroad for me was a way to gain the ability to distinguish the pros from the cons for a successful life's journey. It is not the mere decision to live abroad; it is the understanding of what is best for you and your family and how that can transform into a positive or negative lifestyle. This will depend on your determination. But above all it will require God's intervention and your prayers for God to direct you in your decisions. For me and my family, every step of our decision was backed by God's intervention through our prayers. It was not our own ability only but God's direction that helped us in all aspects of our story and success. Put God first in your planning and decision-making, and believe me, you will have the true conviction that is needed for you and your family.

Discuss things with sincere friends and family members as you move along, but also trust in God for all that you do. I tell you, sometimes it will seem impossible, but if you have the determination and conviction, you will surely succeed and take the right decisions.

Chapter 11

My Country, Sierra Leone

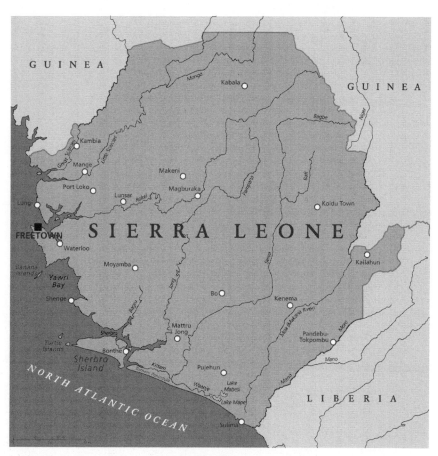

A map of Sierra Leone

Sierra Leone is located on the west coast of Africa, between the 7th and 10th parallels, north of the equator. Sierra Leone is bordered by Guinea to the north and north-east, Liberia to the south and south-east, and the Atlantic Ocean to the west.

Sierra Leone has a total area of 71,740 km² (27,699 sq. mi.), divided into a land area of 71,620 km² (27,653 sq. mi.) and water of 120 km² (46 sq. mi.).

Sierra Leone has four distinct geographical regions: coastal Guinean mangroves, the wooded hill country, an upland plateau, and the eastern mountains. Eastern Sierra Leone is an interior region of large plateaus interspersed with high mountains, where Mount Bintumani rises to 1,948 metres (6,391 ft.).

The history of Sierra Leone began when the land became inhabited by indigenous African peoples at least twenty-five hundred years ago. The dense tropical rainforest partially isolated the region from other West African cultures, and it became a refuge for peoples escaping violence and jihads. Sierra Leone was named by Portuguese explorer Pedro de Sintra, who mapped the region in 1462. The Freetown estuary provided a good natural harbour for ships to shelter in and replenish their drinking water, and it gained more international attention as coastal and transatlantic trade supplanted trans-Saharan trade.

In the mid sixteenth century, the Mane people invaded, subjugated nearly all of the indigenous coastal peoples, and militarized Sierra Leone. The Mane soon blended with the local populations, and the various chiefdoms and kingdoms remained in a continual state of conflict, with many captives sold to European slave traders. The Atlantic slave trade had a significant impact on Sierra Leone, as this trade flourished in the seventeenth and eighteenth centuries. Later Sierra Leone was a centre of antislavery efforts when the trade was abolished in 1807. British abolitionists had organized a colony for black loyalists at Freetown, and this became the capital of British West Africa. A naval squadron was based there to intercept slave ships, and the colony quickly grew as liberated Africans were released, joined by West Indian and African soldiers who had fought for Britain in the Napoleonic Wars.

The descendants of the black settlers were collectively referred to as the Creoles or Krios.

During the colonial era, the British and Creoles increased their control over the surrounding area, securing peace so that commerce would not be interrupted, and suppressing slave trading and interchiefdom war. In 1895, Britain drew borders for Sierra Leone, which they declared to be their protectorate, leading to armed resistance and the Hut Tax War of 1898. Thereafter, there was dissent and reforms as the Creoles sought political rights, trade unions formed against colonial employers, and peasants sought greater justice from their chiefs.

Sierra Leone has played a significant part in modern African political liberty and nationalism. In the 1950s, a new constitution united the crown colony and the protectorate, which had previously been governed separately. Sierra Leone gained independence from the United Kingdom in 1961 and became a member of the Commonwealth of Nations. Ethnic and linguistic divisions remain an obstacle to national unity, with the Mende, Temne, and Creoles as rival power blocs. Roughly half the years since independence have been marked by autocratic governments or civil war.

My Sierra Leone is a beautiful land that we love as demonstrated in our national anthem. The first stanza is amazing and touching: "High we exalt thee, realm of the free. Great is the love we have for thee. Firmly united ever we stand, singing thy praise, O native land. We raise our hearts and our voices on high; the hills and the valleys echo our cry. Blessings and peace be ever thine own, land that we love, our Sierra Leone." What an inspirational national anthem. Sierra Leone is a country rich and endowed with the many types of mineral resources that God has blessed us with. It is definitely a blessed country. People of Sierra Leone are friendly regardless of who you are and where you come from. We like visitors and always make sure they are comfortable and happy. Sometimes we even do so at the expense of our own brothers and sisters.

Despite the problems of civil war, Ebola, and mudslides that the country has faced over the years, some of us are still committed to ensuring that our country develops and becomes a great nation.

The people of Sierra Leone are a resilient people determined to succeed and hopeful that someday Sierra Leone will regain its lost glories. It is important to note that Sierra Leone is made up of decent and tolerant people who interact with each other regardless of tribe or religion. We believe in togetherness, and we stand for each other in times of difficulty. In addition, we believe in supporting each other in times of difficulty. I am always proud of my country and will do all it takes to support it. During my teenage years, I, along with most other young boys and girls of my village, showed discipline, respected my elders, and ensured that I did nothing disrespectful.

It is interesting to note that many of our colleagues who have decided to stay and live in Sierra Leone are living peaceful and stress-free lives. They are making their own contributions towards nation-building. Many are convinced that Sierra Leone needs to develop and grow, so you see a lot of commitment on the part of patriotic Sierra Leoneans for the country to move forward and develop. This is what the country needs, people who are committed and will not turn their backs on or forsake their beloved nation.

A lot of good things can be said about Sierra Leone in terms of culture and values. Even though the country has slowed down over the years in terms of development because of the civil war, at the same time many of the citizens are well convinced that those in positions of trust must put their country first and ensure that the right thing is done to get the country back on its feet. Believe me, Sierra Leone is a fine and excellent country with very nice beaches and wonderful hillside areas where one can admire God's handiwork. Many people who visit Sierra Leone remember the beauty of the country and its people. All that is needed is commitment on the part of all Sierra Leoneans to show love for their country.

Chapter 12

Community Intervention

When I was a teenager, it was my intention to become a lawyer, but somewhere along the line I decided to become a community development professional. This all came about with the many experiences I had acquired after leaving high school and by thinking how I could raise money to support myself and my career. In pursuit of this goal, I was lucky to find myself engaged in several forms of community work in different communities. After working for several years in various communities, I came to the realization that I needed to become a social worker, committed and dedicated to serving poor disadvantaged people the likes of whom I had come across over the years.

I was privileged to have come across so many people—children, youths, women, and men—who involved themselves in different types of work. But the largest segment of those I came across were poor people engaged in petty trading, small-scale farming, and fishing. I worked with many of these people in the communities, and I was amazed and perplexed by some of the things I'd seen and learned. I saw that in some of the communities, people were happy and content with the little they had. Their attitude and their way of life was full of modesty and love for each other. They appreciated whatever help I gave them, and this was accompanied by many thanks and lots of gratitude. I asked myself what was so special about them and why it was that they behaved the way they behaved.

When I interacted with these people, I came to appreciate what I had and what God had given me. Life to these people is togetherness and love. They do things in common and share responsibilities as a community. This means that when there is sadness, they support each other, and when there is joy, they enjoy it together. They are not too mindful of many of the things that we in the city look forward to. The majority of them don't have mobile phones, TVs, or radios. At the same time, they also lack so many things like good clothing, shoes, clean drinking water, and basic health services. But assessing them and looking at their way of life, I discovered that they are happy in their own way. The problems start when we as development professionals go to them and start telling them what they lack and how they need to live. As far as they are concerned, they are happy and content with the little that God has given to them in their various communities.

Most communities actually have their own way of life and of doing things. The culture may be different from one place to the other, but the semblance of being content with what they have is remarkable. I have been doing community work for decades now, and I always admire our community people. In many instances when I have travelled to some of these locations to help with agriculture, health, and income-generation activities, I have observed their behaviours and the manner and way in which they do things. For instance, they go out in the morning to their farms together with some of the children who are not attending school. They farm and return home late in the evening to eat. In almost all cases they eat as a family or in a group as community members. You see the women having their own plates of food. The same is true for the children and men. You see peace of mind and joy in these people at the community level.

Even with only the very basics of life, they are satisfied. This always make me wonder why those of us in the big city want to acquire riches and yet, when we do, we are not happy. Even those who have plenty still want to steal from the poor. They are never satisfied. This is something that has struck me so hard that I tend to emulate some of those fine principles and live a life that is stress-free. These people even have the organic food that we in cities struggle to have. They eat good food and do a lot of exercise. So you find that many of them even live longer than many of us who live in the city. This is a very fine example that we as humans should emulate. We should not be selfish and greedy, which is the biggest problem we have today in most of our countries. Sierra Leone is no exception.

As a community worker, I have all these ideas for how to intervene in the communities to help the people with basic needs such as clean water and good hygiene practices. But on second thought, many of these people do understand what is best for them. They only need genuine support that will improve their lives. The experience they have living in peace and love with one another is something you would be hard-pressed to find in cities and big towns. As community workers we need to tell this good side of the story and emulate the fine example set by many of the people living in these communities.

It is obvious that we, the so-called professionals with all our education, are the ones who confuse these community people by bringing in things that eventually make them vulnerable. The best approach is always for us to have dialogue in the form of workshops or focus group discussions to ascertain what is best for the community and its people. My advice is to encourage our community people not to be reluctant but to continue and ensure that the school runs well. We can also do research on the good things they practise at their level and find out what is most valuable to them that they will need support for.

It's very important that we do not impose on them our own needs and wants just because we have donors who are willing to give money. It is not morally right to do that. This type of practice encourages community separation and weakens that which binds them together as community people. I know that in my years of work, especially working with Plan International, many people who call themselves community workers fail to understand community dynamics and many a time wrongfully do things that hinder the progress of these people. In fact, they end up creating barriers and divisions among them because of the ways in which they approach development issues within those communities.

The people know what is good for them. They have existed for a long time and have built community cohesion and respect for each other. They have the best of green vegetables and plenty of bush meat that they consume. They enjoy their cultures and live a life which is stress-free that many of us do not have the opportunity to have. What is certain is that as community workers we have the responsibility to move in to those communities and evaluate what is good, eliminate what is bad, and see how best we can assist the people. But from my experience, if we choose to condemn all that they do, we are making a big mistake and creating divisions within the community.

I ask that we as community workers be diligent and know what we do when we assist poor, disadvantaged people. It is important not to dictate to them. They already have a happy life. Our goal is to ensure we provide them with additional things that will improve their lives but not take the good things they enjoy as a community away from them. Community togetherness is good therapy and helps people to live long and stress-free lives.

Today many of us have many issues with our health because we strive to own everything we can lay our hands on. We want to have cars, mobile phones, expensive houses, and all the technological and material things we can think of. In the pursuit of getting those things, we end up having too many problems and fall sick to the point that we sometimes end our lives. I think we can learn from our community people who we think are poor. I am certain that they are rich and satisfied in their own way. They don't bother about the many things that we who live in big towns and cities strive for. We worry about too many things and achieve little. So why worry? Let us learn from them. I am sure our lives will be prolonged as a result. According to the Bible, in Matthew 16:26, "What will it profit a man if he should gain the whole world but lose his soul?" Let us appreciate each other and support those who have little. Many of us have a lot, yet we are too selfish and greedy to help others. We can be community people and learn to share and help others. If we do that, Sierra Leone and the world will be a better place.

Chapter 13

Champion Your Dreams

Every human being on earth has a plan for himself or herself or for his or her family. Each person strives to ensure that the future is bright. The entire world in which we live is made up of different people who want to succeed in whatever capacity or career they find themselves. It is the responsibility of individuals to do what is right to ensure they succeed. Our parents are the principal people who have a huge influence over whether or not we succeed as individuals within our society or state. Those who are not fortunate to have their parents with them may have a Good Samaritan, either a family member or family friend, who in some way will come to the rescue and help out. All of us, by whatever means, have come across someone in our lives who has played a vital role in building our success stories. Imagine if we were to put all those stories together, what it would look like. This chapter of my writings is largely focused on me and how my dreams have been realized, taking into consideration those who along the way helped me to realize these all-important dreams.

I am very proud that in all my struggles and throughout my whole life my dreams have been realized, and there are many more to come. It is important to note, though, that I did not achieve them alone. As I was growing up and struggling in life, key people played vital roles to help me realize my dreams. Personally, I had to work hard and be determined to succeed come what may. That determination and commitment was what I demonstrated in order to succeed with the support of others.

It is important to know that you cannot realize your dreams only by hoping and waiting. You must have discipline. For me it was a fight. I struggled in all aspects. Even with all the support I had, if I hadn't had the willingness, seriousness, and determination, it would never have been possible for me to succeed.

I first had to make up my mind that no matter what, I would become the person I wanted to be. I worked very hard, studied, and sacrificed a lot of things, knowing that in the end I would succeed. These sacrifices mean a lot for anyone who wants to champion their dream like me. These sacrifices have to be made in several ways. First, one must not get involved with bad influences. I refused to follow peers who were not of any help or example to me. I determined during my high school days that I wanted to do the things that I knew were right and good for my upbringing. I refused to involve myself in late-night parties when my friends would be off in the corner or elsewhere smoking or drinking alcohol. Rather, I made most of them understand that I had a cause to champion, and that was to succeed in life.

I made sacrifices by not buying too many expensive clothes or other material things. Sometimes I would use a single pair of shoes for the entire two terms just to save money to help my aunt and parents buy other things needed for my schooling. I was determined not to listen to what others said about me. I knew that I needed to be disciplined, and I knew that whatever I was doing, I was doing it to discipline myself. I was engaged in petty trading. At home after school, I would make a local beverage called ginger beer. I would wrap cups of it in small plastic bags that I would put in the freezer for later sale to the public and my neighbours. It was one form of income generation for me that helped support my education. Many of my friends who knew I was engaged in this activity would speak provocative words to me and try to discourage me. I knew exactly what I wanted, and nothing and nobody was going to turn me away from my dreams.

It is worth noting that dreams do not come true just like that. It requires total commitment and hard work to achieve your dreams. I decided that I would only have friends who I believe had the same goals, aims, and dreams as I. At no point did I allow anyone to influence me. Rather, I tried to influence others in a positive way. I wanted my parents and my aunty to be proud of me, so I did all sorts of things to ensure that happened.

In championing your dreams, many a time you will think the road to success is very long and beset by many obstacles. But one thing I was certain of that kept me going was the faith that I had. I depended upon my Lord and Saviour, Jesus Christ. When sometimes I felt down or heartbroken, I would lift my eyes unto my Lord, and he would provide me with strength to see me through. The journey to achieving my dream was long, but at the end of the day I was convinced that I was going to succeed and stand out. I did stand out and eventually succeeded. It was all because of determination, support from parents and guardians, and support from faithful friends and community members.

In pursuing your dreams, you will discover all sort of things, such as those who are committed and those who are not committed to supporting you. You will also discover those who are hypocrites and traitors. All sorts of things will come your way. I had in my mind that come what may, I needed to succeed. Nothing was going to hinder my advancement and progress.

It was during this period that I also came to realize who were my best friends and who were only detractors. It is during this time that you will really discover who will stand by you no matter what you are going through. It was during this time that I came to realize those friends and people who were hypocrites and who were only there for me because of what they were getting from me. And when what I was giving them ceased coming, those people quit. It was during this time that I truly came to understand that your sisters and brothers do not necessarily live under the same roof or share the same blood as you. Rather, they are those who will make sacrifices and stand by you in times of trial and tribulation. It was during this time that I discovered that human beings are not to be trusted and that God is the only one you can put your trust in. It was during this time that I came to my senses and understood that there are evil people in the workplace, and many of them are your alleged close friends. But the good thing is that God is always there as my protector and the one who can be trusted regardless of who is against me.

To champion your dream as I did requires dedication and perseverance. It requires good heart and selfless sacrifice for others. It requires meeting new people, discussing and sharing what is positive to get you going. It also requires being humble and treating everyone you meet with respect and dignity regardless of where these people come from, who they are, or what they look like. It means giving and even sacrificing the little you have. I have seen it all, and I have come to appreciate myself and my family.

To champion your dreams means having a wife and children who will be there for you when all seems lost. It means having children and a wife who understand that life is not all about your family but that it is also about others. My family understands that, and they support me in many ways to achieve my dreams. If you need to champion your dreams, you need to understand that the world is not equal and there are those who need you and want your support as well. Don't ever ignore this if you feel the need to succeed in life. Believe that if you save the lives of others and bring change to them, you will receive your blessings from God almighty. We cannot achieve our dreams when others are suffering. I succeeded in my dreams because I wanted others to succeed too. I have seen a lot of people who are just too selfish and want every good thing for themselves and their families.

Achieving your dreams does not mean being selfish and greedy or proud. I have seen friends and colleagues who are proud and do not even want to associate themselves with those they believe are not their type. I championed my dreams and ended up becoming successful in life because all those I came across, I tried in my own way to touch so that they too could be useful to those they came across. If people in the world would touch each other, the suffering and poverty that we have today would be eradicated. But I have seen the worst, how many people in my own country deliberately treat their own brothers and sisters negatively. They only think about themselves and their families, forgetting that the world is a global village and that we are all the same on one planet. I successfully championed my dream because I wanted others to arrive at their goals too.

I don't want, and I have never wanted, to end up at the goal alone. I wanted to be able to celebrate with others so that many people could be touched and then go out and reach a goal with many more people. It makes no sense if you reach the goal alone. You will not have anyone else near you to celebrate with. God has given each of us talents and skills to motivate others. Let us champion our dreams and bring others along with us. Having others along will mean sacrificing many things in life. It will mean having to spend time with those who are poor, those who are distressed, those with little faith, and those who are in total despair. It will mean making yourself available to others when they need you, ensuring that you set a good example and are disciplined. It will mean being truthful and sincere with your friends and those whom you mingle with. It will mean doing things right, especially in your community and country so that development can be realized. It will mean ensuring that you set a good example when you work in public places and serve those you have been destined to serve. I have been blessed, and today I still enjoy the journey that started many years ago with many people who followed me on the path.

It was hard starting the race. I encountered many hurdles and frustrations, and sometimes I felt like quitting, but I was determined with the support of others I came across on the way to succeed in my dreams. Never give up, and never see yourself as a failure. God has a plan for each one of us. If you are determined, you can rest assured that you will succeed. Today I can do many things that I could not afford to do along my journey. I could not afford to buy many shoes, clothes, etc. Today I can buy whatever I want, including cars, shoes, and clothes. The list can go on and on. But the reality is that even in your dreams, you should continue to reach others and make a difference. Allow yourself the opportunity to start a journey, knowing that it is not going to be easy. Understand that a lot of challenges and turbulence will come. But be ready to face these problems. You will come across detractors and people who are jealous, but stand firm and believe, and above all know that with God all things are possible.

Printed and bound by PG in the USA